U.S.-CARIBBEAN RELATIONS

Their Impact on Peoples and Culture

Edited by
Ransford W. Palmer

PRAEGER

Westport, Connecticut
London

Library of Congress Cataloging-in-Publication Data

U.S.-Caribbean relations : their impact on peoples and culture /
edited by Ransford W. Palmer.
    p. cm.
  Includes bibliographical references and index.
  ISBN 0-275-95859-0 (alk. paper)
    1. Caribbean Area—Civilization—American influences.
2. Caribbean Area—Economic conditions—1945-   3. Caribbean
Area—Relations—United States. 4. United States—Relations—Caribbean
Area. I. Palmer, Ransford W.
F2169.U6 1998
303.48′2729073—dc21   96-53610

British Library Cataloguing in Publication Data is available.

Library of Congress Catalog Card Number: 96-53610
ISBN: 0-275-95859-0

First published in 1998

Praeger Publishers, 88 Post Road West, Westport, CT 06881
An imprint of Greenwood Publishing Group, Inc.

Printed in the United States of America

The paper used in this book complies with the
Permanent Paper Standard issued by the National
Information Standards Organization (Z39.48–1984).

10 9 8 7 6 5 4 3 2 1

Contents

Acknowledgments

The chapters in this book are based on papers selected from those presented in April 1996 at the conference on U.S.-Caribbean relations, which I organized in my capacity as the Associate Director for Research at the Ralph J. Bunche International Affairs Center at Howard University. I am grateful to the Center for sponsoring the conference and to its director, Howard G. Dawson, Jr., for his support. I am also grateful to Lena Gibson for being so reliable and good natured; to Dana Heyliger for helping us out of difficult situations; and to the members of the conference planning committee, John Cotman, Wilfred David, Linda Heywood, Ivor Livingston, and Vincent McDonald, for their constructive input. A special appreciation also goes to senior productions editor Catherine A. Lyons of the Greenwood Publishing Group for her meticulous work on the manuscript.

1

An Overview

Ransford W. Palmer

The theme of these chapters is the impact of U.S.-Caribbean relations on the lives of the peoples of the Caribbean. The impact is economic as well as cultural, social, and political. It involves the massive movement of people side by side with the movement of goods and services. It also involves the shaping of aspirations and the struggle to create and preserve an identity that fires people's imaginations to realize their aspirations.

The United States looms large in the lives of Caribbean peoples. Although most of these countries have had a long history of European colonialism, their European heritage is constantly being eroded by their growing dependence on the North American economy and by their naked exposure to the power of North American telecommunications.

This volume begins with an historical perspective of the social aspect of U.S.-Caribbean relations since World War II by Fitzroy Baptiste, with particular emphasis on the role of race and ethnocentrism. Even before World War II, Baptiste argues, "The United States began to evince an extension of her influence, even ownership over the 'odds and ends' of European-owned Caribbean and Atlantic islands." Baptiste sees the Caribbean today as balkanized and dominated by external powers. This domination and subordination theme is reflected in race relations where a "pigmentocracy of whites, neowhites, Chinese, Jews and Syrian-Lebanese" control economic power. Baptiste argues that "as the United States, with its historically sharp white-black sociology, penetrated the circum-Caribbean in this century, one sociological result has been the reinforcing of the pigment line in circum-Caribbean countries." Baptiste sees the explosion of the American-dominated tourism as a major instrument in this process.

More troubling for the Caribbean in Baptiste's eyes is what he calls "the pervasive commoditization and consumption of the United States way of life via cable television and other instruments." He observes that this process is also encouraged by the growth of Caribbean migration to the United States. But he also acknowledges that this migration has had an important sociocultural impact on American life, especially in the area of music and literature.

Part II of the book examines population movements between the United States and the Caribbean. In Chapter 3, Jay R. Mandle focuses on the centrality of tourism and migration in the economic development of the Caribbean. Mandle suggests that these population flows "have created a relationship that has influenced each side more than is typically the result of conventional bilateral relations." He identifies two major benefits from these population flows. One is that the tourism industry allows the Caribbean to benefit from its comparative advantage in location, salubrious climate, and great beaches; and the other is the safety valve that migration has provided. Mandle acknowledges that emigration "undermine[s] hopes for economic development" but believes that this is "an unintended consequence of rational market behavior." He also believes that investment in education is critical for the development of the region even though some educated workers will be lost to migration.

In Chapter 4, Ransford W. Palmer picks up Mandle's population flows theme. The counterflows of tourists and immigrants, Palmer argues, are principally the result of the much higher level of income in the United States. Population flows from the Caribbean to the United States also includes temporary visitors for pleasure who are in fact tourists. The composition of the flow of immigrants and temporary visitors to the United States also depends on the level of income in the sending country. Using the example of Trinidad and Tobago during the oil prosperity of the 1970s, Palmer demonstrates the positive relationship between the composition of the population flows and the level of income. That is to say, as income rises, the share of temporary visitors (tourists) in the population outflow rises. This leads to the hypothesis that the process of economic development in the Caribbean is one that transforms Caribbean immigrants into tourists. Like Mandle, Palmer sees the migration of the Caribbean household as a rational behavior because the household seeks to maximize future household income that facilitates greater investment in their children's education. In his theoretical framework, immigrant remittances play the dual role of providing large amounts of foreign exchange for the country of origin and being an indicator of the completeness or incompleteness of the household migration process.

In Chapter 5, Curtis Ward looks at the future of U.S. immigration policy. He begins with the premise that "immigration legislation in the United States reflects the prevailing economic and political conditions of the day." Ward provides an historical account of two distinct patterns of U.S. immigration policy: an open-door policy prior to 1875 and a trend of ever-increasing restrictions since. He examines the mandate of the U.S. Commission on Immigration reform and its recommendations regarding family unification, labor requirements, and other issues. Ward expects that the attitude of U.S. politicians toward immigration will be governed by the extent to which legal immigration is seen to pose a real threat to the majority population "both in terms of its composition with regard to ethnicity and race" and also by the extent to which "civic participation by immigrants, as they become citizens, could invariably affect the political landscape one way or another." And he feels certain that in the future the United States will put pressure on Caribbean Basin countries to pursue economic policies aimed at reducing the propensity of Caribbean people to migrate to the United States.

Part III of the book focuses on the cultural dimensions of U.S.-Caribbean relations. In Chapter 6, Joyce Toney looks at Caribbean Americans in New York City and explores the phenomenon of the export of Caribbean culture, especially in the areas of music and carnivals. Toney focuses on the West Indian Carnival in Brooklyn,

New York, which is held each year on Labor Day. She sees two kinds of benefits accruing to the Caribbean community from the Carnival. One is the financial benefits to the Carnival organizers and entrepreneurs, and the other is the "increased political clout" that the Carnival represents.

Errol Miller, in Chapter 7, differentiates the Caribbean from the cultural panorama of the Americas and identifies four important differences: first, the region's European connection being far more diverse than Latin America's; second, the virtual nonexistence of the culture of the first inhabitants; third, the interaction of the various European cultures with African and Indian peoples; and fourth, the Caribbean being the only region outside of Africa where people of African ancestry constitute the majority. Miller argues that Caribbean uniqueness and diversity "present their own peculiar challenges to unity, integration, and cooperation" by fostering "a tendency to look outside the region for paradigms of action."

Miller sees the new Association of Caribbean States (ACS) creating an even wider diversity in the Caribbean because it "attempts to bring mestizo America into formal relationship with Plantation America in this geographical intersection between the North and South of the hemisphere." Though the intent of the ACS is to promote greater economic integration of the region, Miller sees the weak intraregional cultural links as a significant obstacle toward this goal. Yet he is optimistic that "the greatest long-term prospects offered by the ACS appears to be in the area of culture and not economics." This optimism rests on the fact that although the Caribbean exists on the periphery of wealth, power, and status in the hemisphere, it is the geographic center of the Americas, and that "the ACS, by bringing into association the different cultural streams of the hemisphere, opens the prospect that one day they may flow into a single river." Miller hopes that this cultural stream will also bring ideas and ideals that will transform the paradigms of the past and transport the marginalized peoples of the Caribbean toward greater political and economic well-being.

In Chapter 8, Merle Collins examines perceptions of culture and sovereignty in the Caribbean. Collins's idea of culture and sovereignty suggests, among other things, "that the culture (ideas, values) of other nations do not become more important than its own in the shaping of its sense of self." But this sense of self is constantly under attack from American commercial television, which promotes the American way of consumption to peoples with low incomes. Drawing on the Caribbean film, *And the Dish Ran Away with the Spoon,* a Banyan production for a BBC program on Development Studies, Collins underscores the pervasive influence of American television programming in the Caribbean. She argues that because Caribbean countries are small and live in the shadow of the collossus to the north, their cultural attitudes have been influenced by a "sense of socioeconomic and cultural vulnerability." But their sense of self need not be eroded if they take themselves and their culture seriously.

In Chapter 9, *Religious Imperatives in Caribbean Development: The U.S. Connection,* Kortright Davis addresses a dimension of U.S.-Caribbean relations that is often neglected. Davis introduces the importance of religion in the lives of Caribbean people through music. Among other things, he points out that music "liberates them from despair and from pretensions of superiority and intimidation. It sweetens the fabric of physical work, reinforces social upliftment, and energizes the practice of spiritual worship. Music, to be sure, is the Caribbean voice of God." Davis traces the two parallel lines of the Caribbean religious experience: the formally established churches and the various groupings within Islam, Hinduism, and Judaism on the one hand, and the indigenous religions that owe their genesis to their African heritage on the other. The churches began with the settlement of the planter classes but in the course of time threw off the vestiges of colonial domination and dependence and assumed "a radically different role in the transformation of society." Davis underscores the important role of the contemporary Caribbean church and its linkage with the Caribbean diaspora in promoting social change "in the face of some endemic oppressive realities."

In the final chapter, James Early's aim is to sensitize the reader regarding the cultural sterility of the neo-liberal economic language that shapes our understanding of globalization today. This language, he argues, obscures the history and culture of those it describes as workers and consumers. Early sees regionalization as leading to the devaluation of indigenous culture and fears that the positive relationship between culture and economic development may be undermined by the creation of the ACS. Early is convinced that "when international relations are pursued without sufficient regard for cultural and social factors, the souls and spirits of everyday people are too often crushed and reconstituted into mechanical cogs of an ever-expanding economic system that values them only, or mostly, as commodities, then despises their moral and social behaviors." For Early, indigenous Caribbean culture is essential to the economic development of the people. It not only enriches their quality of life, it preserves their identity by serving as a buffer against the onslaught of homogenization that globalization encourages.

These chapters raise profound questions about the identity and the destiny of Caribbean peoples as their countries move inexorably into the economic and cultural sphere of the United States. The interaction of Caribbean and American peoples through tourism and migration, the movement of goods and services, and the selling of the American life-style on television constantly threaten Caribbean cultural identity. But if political leaders make cultural development an integral part of their development strategy, these same threats can be transformed into sources of indigenous cultural vigor.

2

United States-Caribbean Relations from World War II to the Present: The Social Nexus

Fitzroy A. Baptiste

INTRODUCTION

This book examines the changing relations between the congeries in the global system and its Western Hemisphere's subsystem in the period of the 1980s to the present boundary of the twenty first century. The two congeries are, on the one hand, the United States of America, today the sole Superpower in the global system and, for a century or so, the "colossus" in the Western Hemisphere; and, on the other hand, a periphery of the United States called the Caribbean.

More specifically, I have been asked to write about the "social nexus" of the relations between these two congeries: from World War II to the present. There is difficulty with this narrow time-boundary. As anyone knows, the time-boundary of the United States' expansion in to the Caribbean (also the Pacific) and the resultant "social nexus" extends further than 1945 to this day. The later period is a continuum from at least the late nineteenth century. In turn, U.S. expansionism in the Caribbean was preceded by that of earlier powers—Western European (Spain, France, the Netherlands, Britain). Boundaries in history are merely convenient tools used by historians for research and writing. We must remember, however, that history is about process: one stage leading to another.

This brings me to the sense of the term "social nexus." My sense is that of the colonial/imperial situation, that is, the range of unequal relations that have developed in the process of modern imperialism from the fifteenth century between North Atlantic Powers, including the the United States, on the one hand, and weaker countries in the New World, Africa and Asia, on the other hand, as the former intruded state power into the spheres of the latter. The inequalities that derived from this process of history cover the gamut of military, political, diplomatic, economic, social/sociological, cultural, and psychological variables. A tall order. An important variable, however, in any discussion of the "social nexus" or "the colonial situation" in post-fifteenth century North Atlantic imperialisms is that of *race* and *ethnocentrism*: from the empirical fact that the imperialists/colonizers were of the Caucasian/white "race" and the colonized mainly non-white races.

This theme of race and ethnocentrism will pervade my discussion not only of U.S.-Caribbean relations from the late nineteenth century but the historico-sociological antecedents from the fifteenth century. My interest in African history, African and other diaspora studies, and U.S.-Caribbean relations takes me to this theme instinctively. In doing so, I am conscious that I may invade the "history" boundary of Professor Franklin Knight or the "economics" focus of Professor Jay Mandle. This is inevitable. Indeed, some of the themes that I have selected to discuss—such as tourism, narco-trafficking, and narco-diplomacy; the growing commoditization of the American way of life in the Caribbean via cable TV and other forms; and, the other side of the nexus, the growing immigration of Caribbean peoples to the United States since 1945 and their sociocultural impact on American life—will invade slightly the spheres of other papers presented in this text. It is a matter of balance and of the interdisciplinary perspective that must prevail.

I have structured this paper into two parts: firstly, my preamble of the historical process from the late fifteenth century that culminated in U.S. domination of the Caribbean from 1870; and, secondly and relatedly, aspects of the "social nexus" as indicated. One is conscious that the "social nexus" aspects are wider than the ones identified. One would have liked to tap literature to see what light it throws on the "social nexus." Also the discussion is more on the Anglo/Commonwealth Caribbean than on the other "Caribbeans," because I know more about the former.

DEFINITION OF "THE CARIBBEAN"

Though the geopolitical definition of the United States is clear, that of "the Caribbean" requires definition upfront. For the purpose of this paper, "Caribbean" is defined as *both* the archipelagic chain of small republics and other islands in the Western Atlantic and the Caribbean Sea from Bermuda and the Bahamas in the north close to the eastern seaboard of the United States thence to Trinidad and Tobago and Barbados in the south and east proximate to continental South America; *and* the circum or rimlands of American Florida, Mexican Yucatan, the Isthmus of Central America, Colombia, Venezuela, and the Guyanas (ex-British/Cooperative Republic of Guyana; ex-Dutch/Suriname; and colonial French Guiana). This definition conforms to that of most experts in the field of U.S.-Caribbean-Latin American relations.[1]

Undoubtedly, the significant geopolitical variable of the "Caribbean" as defined here is its mini-entity configuration, with the exception of Mexico, Colombia, and Venezuela, vis-à-vis the United States. The only other archipelagic part of the world that approaches the Caribbean in its composition of mini-states is the South Pacific.

Our geopolitical definition of Caribbean suggests a unity. In a historico-sociological sense, however, there is not one Caribbean but several Caribbeans, namely British/Commonwealth; Spanish/Hispanic; French; Dutch; and ex-Danish/now United States. The United States-held Caribbean also includes today the ex-Spanish colony of Puerto Rico.

Linguistically, the peoples of the archipelago and the rimland of the Caribbean are English- (including American English), Spanish-, French-, and Dutch-speaking mainly, with a number of so-called "Creole" dialects that reflect the interaction between these European languages and those of native Indians and incoming continental Africans and Asians from the late fifteenth century.

The preceding is our way of saying that the contemporary historico-sociological diversity of the circum-Caribbean has been shaped by the entry of Western Europe into the Western Hemisphere, Africa, and Asia in the "First Imperialism" from c1450 to 1870. The Western Hemisphere and, within it, the circum-Caribbean, was partitioned between and among competing Western European Powers (Spain; Portugal; Britain; France; the Netherlands; Denmark; and, for a time, Baltic states) and linked vertically into their respective mercantile economies. In turn, the economies were based on the exploitation of New World mineral resources and agro-commodities that used native Indian serf-, African slave-, and Asian indentured-labor mainly between 1492 and into the nineteenth century.

EUROPEAN DOMINATION OF THE CARIBBEAN: 1492 TO c1870

The history of the strategic value of the Caribbean is rich and varied. We begin with a brief look at European domination of the area.[2]

In the classic era of the wooden ships of the line and frigates up to the early nineteenth century, the Caribbean Zone became endowed with a high geostrategic ranking as stations for the war and merchant navies of competing European powers. "Sea power," defined in terms of the superiority of the national Navy and of the national maritime commerce, held the key to dominance. The Caribbean became the classic theater of rivalry and warfare between and among European Powers as each tried to establish a mare clausum. For a century and more from the early sixteenth century, Spanish sea power guarded the Caribbean island-chain as the route from the rich American bullion mines to Europe. In turn, Spain was challenged in the Caribbean and displaced to some extent by her European rivals—England, France, and the Netherlands.

The geostrategic importance of the Caribbean as naval stations and communication keys in relation to the Americas and Euro-Africa was underlined in the wars for naval-cum-maritime supremacy between the Dutch and the English in the second half of the seventeenth century, and between the English and the French from the late seventeenth century into the early nineteenth century. Indicative of the command-of-the-seas strategy of naval warfare then and of the importance of the Caribbean in that strategy, both the British and French Grand Fleets raced across the Atlantic to try and sever each other's arteries, in the buildup to the decisive Battle of Trafalgar in 1805 during the Napoleonic and Revolutionary "World War."

The Peace of Vienna underwrote the new international order after that conflict and recognized Britain as the dominant power in the Caribbean and the Western Hemisphere. By that date, however, a new power was emerging to challenge Britain and to displace her ultimately as the dominant one in the Western Hemisphere. We refer to the United States, one of a number of new states that arose in the Western Hemisphere via national liberation struggles against the European imperialisms.

For about a century after the United States' war of independence against Britain, the relations between the two English-speaking countries were schizophrenic. The Monroe Doctrine of 1823 enunciated the pretensions of the new United States to primacy in the Western Hemisphere against Britain and all of Europe. It was British sea power, however, that gave credibility to the Monroe Doctrine and protected the United States and the other hemispheric new states from the rest of Europe. Simultaneously, British and U.S. strategic planning targeted each other as the main "enemy" in the Atlantic: on account of Canada and the issue of the future construction of an isthmian canal in Central America to bridge the Atlantic-Caribbean to the Pacific and the Indian Ocean.

THE RISE TO DOMINANCE OF THE CIRCUM-CARIBBEAN BY THE UNITED STATES: c1870

The period from c1870 to 1945 witnessed the explosive assertion by the United States of her specific and predominant interest in the circum-Caribbean, as well as in the Pacific, in displacement of Britain as well as Spain, France, the Netherlands, and Denmark (for the circum-Caribbean). The indices of this process in the circum-Caribbean included:

1. The Panama Canal Zone (PCZ), located within the confines of a new Central American republic that was carved out of the national territory

of Colombia. It became the keystone of a so-called "American Lake" strategic triangle in the region (Child 1979, 1980).

2. The two other components of the "American Lake"[3] conceptualization comprised Cuba and Puerto Rico to the north and east of the PCZ. Both were acquired and dominated by the United States, as a result of military victory over Spain in the Spanish-American War of 1898. Puerto Rico, with the adjacent Culebra and Vieques Islands, was an outright acquisition. On the other hand, Cuba gained her independence from Spain by an Act of the United States Congress. The new republic was imposed on from the outset by a series of unequal treaties which, inter alia, gave the base rights to the United States at the site of Guantanamo Bay *in perpetuo*.

3. The "American Lake" line was stretched east of Puerto Rico-Culebra-Vieques in 1917 by the purchase of the Danish West Indies in order to forestall Germany. The new acquisition was renamed the United States (US) Virgin Islands.

4. The extension by 1918 of an Occupation of the Dominican Republic and Haiti and a virtual Protectorate over Nicaragua. The United States concluded the Bryan-Chamorro Treaty with Nicaragua, which secured for the United States the monopoly grant in perpetuity over any probable alternative or complementary Canal route across Nicaragua to link the Pacific with the Caribbean Sea.

The raison d'être of the acquisition of the U.S. Virgin Islands was both to enhance a "Puerto Rico-Narragansett Bay Line," inclusive of Long Island Sound, Block Island Sound, Vineyard Sound, and Massachusetts Bay on the United States' East Coast, but also the strategic line east into the Caribbean Sea and the Atlantic Ocean. This redefinition was called the Quarter-sphere. By 1945 it developed into the full Hemisphere Defense conceptualization.

The Quarter-sphere embraced an area from Alaska to the Galapagos Islands, off Pacific Peru, thence to the bulge of Brazil, thence to Newfoundland, off Atlantic Canada, and thence back to Alaska. The "Hemisphere" came to include, in the Atlantic Ocean, Iceland, Greenland, and the Faroes, which were the link between Northern Europe and Canada; as well as the Cape Verdes, the Canaries, and the Azores. It also came to embrace the entire archipelago of the Caribbean Sea and the Western Atlantic. In the words of a 1918 document of the General Board of the U.S. Navy, the definition included "all odds and ends of territories."[4] These "odds and ends of territories" in the wider arc of the Caribbean Sea and the Atlantic Ocean towards Euro-Africa were then owned by European Colonial Powers, including Britain, Denmark, the Netherlands, Portugal, and Spain.

The United States began to evince an extension of her influence, even ownership, over these "odds and ends" of European-owned Caribbean and Atlantic islands between 1918 and 1939. In the circum-Caribbean, the 1918–1939 indices of the growing U.S. interest included the following:

1. In the airline field, the virtual-monopoly extension of the US Pan American Airways (PAA) into the Caribbean, Central America and South America.

2. The Flying Boat, the hydro-aeroplane, and the catapult—all of them essential mechanisms in the process of harnessing aviation for sea operations—began to take shape in the model basin of the Washington Navy Yard. By 1916 the new experimental battleship, the U.S.S. *North Carolina*, was using aeroplanes and kite balloons, was fitted with catapults, and had on board the latest four types of aircraft that had been developed for sea work. In addition, eight other armored cruisers were being fitted, and scout cruisers were being designed to carry aircraft. By 1929 the concept of the Fast Carrier Task Force, which was to play such a vital role in Atlantic and Pacific theaters of World War II, had been worked out. The laboratory was the Annual Fleet War Games of the Naval War College. The Caribbean Sea near the PCZ was a major locus operandi.

3. The push for bases in the British, French and Dutch Caribbean; and even a lobby in the U.S. Congress and the U.S. Navy Department to get the United States to purchase Caribbean territories from the European powers in part settlement of World War I debts. In this regard, World War I and the interwar years saw a series of reports on the subject of the United States' needs for bases in the Caribbean, the Atlantic, and the Pacific. They included the Baker, Cox, Oliver, and White Reports by 1918; and the Helm Board Report and the Hepburn Board Report of 1930 and 1938, respectively.

AIRCRAFT AND SUBMARINE AS THE FIRST ICBMs

Why all of this and more by the United States vis-à-vis the circum-Caribbean by 1939? As I have argued, these developments derived to some extent from the United States' response to the advent of the oil-combustion-engine aircraft and submarine as new instruments of warfare between 1913 and 1939, themselves parts of a wider scientific-technological revolution that included tele-communications (wireless and telephone) and automatic guns and other weapons.

In retrospect, we can see the aircraft and the submarine as the first generation of today's intercontinental ballistic missiles (ICBMs). By introducing, for the first time in World War I, a long-range, rapid-movement, and greater combat-radius to war-fare, the aircraft and the submarine threatened to shrink consid-erably the degree of security that, until then, oceans such as the Atlantic and the Pacific afforded to the United States. The United States and the entire Western Hemisphere now became bridge-able via the stepping-stones of the Atlantic and Pacific islands; across narrow seas as the Bering Straits; the great circle of the North Atlantic/Arctic; and the Straits of Dakara from West Africa to the bulge of Brazil.

One diplomatic-naval response was the rapprochement be-tween the United States and Britain in order to counter Germany and Japan on the Atlantic and the Pacific fronts. The alliance, with France and others, stood the test of World War I—just barely. Another major response by the United States was the further stretching of the strategic line far-forward of her landmass into the outer Caribbean, the Atlantic, and the Pacific in order to take cognizance of the new air-sea realities—that is, the concept of far-advanced bases or a sort of U.S. Maginot Line.

Admiral Alfred Thayer Mahan gave one of the earliest articula-tions of the far-advanced-base concept via the naval War College between 1884 and his death in 1914, that is, just before the age of the deployment of the aircraft and the submarine in World War I. With the lessons of the war before them, including the near sever-ance of the British-French supply lines from the Americas by Ger-many, we find Lt. Commander Virgil Baker, U.S. Navy District Communication Superintendent in Puerto Rico, writing:

That theory of strategy which provides that Naval bases necessary for the outposts of Naval battle lines shall be advanced as far as possible to the front has been strengthened by the facts brought by the European war and by the wide development of the means and the increase in the efficiency of Naval scouting. It has become almost an axiom that there is no other consideration so formidable and serious to an invading fleet as that of a securely-defended and well-equipped naval base possessed by the country to be invaded and situated at a position well advanced to the front beyond the objective of the invading fleet.[5]

Likewise, the General Board of the U.S. Navy Department had this to say concerning the future role of United States naval aviation within the new far-advanced-base strategy:

To insure air supremacy, to enable the United States navy to meet on at least equal terms any possible enemy, and to put the United States in its proper place as a naval power, fleet aviation must be developed to the fullest possible extent. Aircraft must become an essential arm of the fleet. A naval air service must be established, capable of accompanying and operating with the fleet in all waters of the globe.[6]

These articulations of the United States' strategy in the age of the then "new warfare" emanated from new, technologically-oriented centers within the Navy Department. The centers included the Office of the Chief of Naval Operations (1915) and the Bureau of Aeronautics (1921).

If we grasp the selective pressures exerted by the aircraft and the submarine on the security of the United States between 1914 and 1918, the indices of the growth of the United States' interest in the circum-Caribbean between 1918 and 1939 should become understandable. So, too, the growth of "Dollar Diplomacy" or the faster penetration of trans-national corporation (TNCs) investments of the United States in the countries of the circum-Caribbean and the wider Hemisphere.

The investments took in what a 1928 document of the British Committee of Imperial Defence termed "certain raw materials" vital to "a successful issue from a modern war" and "obtainable only from certain localities." By 1939 the "certain raw materials" numbered 35, including 3 located in the circum-Caribbean, namely bauxite for aircraft production; petroleum, the new fuel factor; and mica for the manufacture of radio and radar condensers, aircraft megneto condensers, radio tubes, spark plugs, electric motors, generators, and transformers.

By 1939 British and Dutch Guianas ranked as one of the world's largest producers of bauxite, with the industry controlled by a United States-Canadian TCN known as the Aluminum Company of America (ALCOA) and a Canadian offshoot, the Aluminum Company of Canada (ALCAN). The ALCOA-ALCAN bauxite mines of the Guianas supplied the United States alone with about 50 percent of her needs at the outbreak of World War II.

In oil producing and oil refining, the circum-Caribbean Mexico, Colombia, Venezuela, British Trinidad, and Dutch Aruba and Curaçao ranked high in the global tables: again with the United States taking most of the exports. Here again, the industry was controlled by a number of U.S. TNCs such as Standard Oil Company of New Jersey and Gulf Oil, with stakes by British and Dutch interests also. Cuba became an important source of mica, with the sector controlled by U.S. interests.[7]

The momentum of U.S. penetration into the circum-Caribbean from the late nineteenth century into the first two decades of the twentieth century reached a peak during World War II. Then, all the countries of the circum-Caribbean, independent and non-independent, "came to constitute part of a United States-defined hemispheric security system" against the Axis powers. In turn, this hemispheric system was interlocked into the United States-led and Allied global defensive/offensive system against the Axis. The United States established a base presence in the British West Atlantic and Caribbean territories of Newfoundland, Bermuda; the Bahamas, Jamaica, Antigua, St. Lucia, Trinidad, and British Guiana under the 1940–1941 Destroyers-Bases Agreement with Britain. She occupied the Dutch territories of Aruba, Curaçao, and Dutch Guiana/Suriname to secure the vital oil and bauxite for the Allied war effort, in diplomatic arrangements with Venezuela and Brazil. When the French Caribbean territories of Martinique, Guadeloupe, and French Guiana became a threat to the security interests of the Allies by their adherence to the Vichy, pro-German Government of Marshal Pétain between mid-1940 and 1943, the United States clamped a virtual Protectorate over them. Relatedly, Mexico, the Central American states (with the PCZ as a key), Colombia, Venezuela, the Dominican Republic, Haiti, and, of course, Puerto Rico and the U.S. Virgins Islands were locked into the Allied carapace.[8]

REPOSITIONING THE CIRCUM-CARIBBEAN
AGAINST THE THREAT OF THE U.S.S.R.-LED
COMMUNIST BLOC: 1947 TO THE 1980s

By 1947 the United States and her West European allies had come to see the "Communist" U.S.S.R., ally against the Axis powers in World War II, as the new threat to their global security interest, in a context of *decolonization* in the Caribbean, Africa, and Asia. The United States' assessment of the threat of the U.S.S.R to herself and her allies is evident in a General Operation Plan No. 47 of the United States Atlantic Fleet dated 10 September 1947. The plan stated: The U.S.S.R. is the world power whose political and economic objectives conflict in the greatest degree with those of the United States. As the U.S.S.R. is the most probable enemy of the United States, it is possible that war between the United States and the U.S.S.R. can be precipitated because of an incident or as a result of a premeditated military action by the U.S.S.R. to achieve her national aims. The satellite countries of the U.S.S.R. will contribute their economic and manpower resources.[9]

Moreover, the assessment of the U.S.S.R threat to Western interests took cognizance that yet another age of warfare had entered: intercontinental ballistic missiles or ICBMs. As happened in the first stage of the ICBMs in the forms of aircraft and submarines, U.S. planners moved to "new-model" existing security systems and to fashion new ones—fitting the Caribbean and the Western Hemisphere in.

The North Atlantic Treaty Organization (NATO) was established in 1947, as a "new-modeling" of the World War II Grand Alliance, with the United States maintaining her role of leadership. The Organization of American States (OAS), established by the Rio Treaty of Reciprocal Assistance of 1947, emerged as the Western Hemisphere subsystem of NATO. Its members included the United States and all the independent republics in Latin America, including those in the circum-Caribbean. Next, some of these archipelagic republics and dependencies of Britain were locked by the NATO powers into their global ICBM counter to the threat of the U.S.S.R. In some cases, World War II bases that had been acquired by the United States in British and non-British archipelagic territories were turned over to the ICBM-system. For example, on 11 May

1949, President Truman signed a bill authorizing the expenditure of $75 million to establish a 3,000-mile ICBM testing ground from Florida into the Caribbean Sea and the Atlantic Ocean. It was envisaged that the testing of the flight of the ICBMs would require the establishment of radar tracking stations in the Caribbean and the Atlantic. Some of those stations would be on "picketboats;" some would be shorebased. There ensued a new-modeling of the Caribbean-Atlantic carapace of World War II as follows:

1. U.S.-British Agreement of 1949–1950 for the establishment of a long range proving ground (LRPG) in the Bahamas.
2. A 1952 agreement between the two powers extending the Bahamas LRPG to the Turks and Caicos Islands.
3. The further extension of the LRPG to include Antigua, St. Lucia, and Trinidad as well as the Dominican Republic and Ascension Island by 1960.

Additionally, Barbados and the Turks and Caicos became the locations of "oceanographic research stations," within a naval program of oceanographic research "designed to acquire and evaluate fundamental data of a general defense interest relating to water conditions" and to develop techniques and equipment for acquiring such data from shore-based stations and for the training of personnel. Finally, a LORAN (long range aid for navigation) station was established in Jamaica in 1959. We see in all this some of the measures taken by the United States, by agreement with the relevant governments, to refit the Caribbean to take account of the coming of the missile of warfare and strategy.

In turn, these developments reinforced the importance of Caribbean oil, bauxite, and other resources to the United States and her allies. According to the Secretary of the Air Force in his annual report for July 1, 1962, to June 30, 1963, the U.S. consumption of strategic raw materials was to rise by 90 percent between 1950 and 1975. It required more than twice as much aluminum in 1962 to produce a jet fighter plane as it did in 1945: 9,273 pounds in 1945 and 19,440 pounds in 1962.

Accordingly, the United States acted in the postwar years, as in World War II, to fit the oil, bauxite, etc., of the Caribbean and Western Hemisphere into her stockpiling of strategic raw materials to take account of the Cold War and, especially, the Korean War. U.S. stockpiling policy then emphasized, as it does today, exploitation of available overseas sources of raw materials in order to conserve domestic resources. The Caribbean, given its geographical position, has been given a high strategic ranking by the postwar NATO system, as by its World War II precursor, as a rich source of oil and bauxite. During the Korean War, the Central Intelligence Agency took special measures to protect the bauxite mines in Suriname; and the oil-producing and refining continuum of the Eastern Caribbean. The Navy and the War Departments apparently reentered some leased bases in the British Caribbean, such as the Chaguaramas base in Trinidad.

Of course, the United States engaged in a number of gunboat interventions in the circum-Caribbean in the Cold War. It acted clandestinely to overthrow an alleged Communist regime in Guatemala in 1954. Later in the 1970s-1980s, it acted against the Sandinista, "leftist" regime in Nicaragua. It subverted the communists and independentistas in its colony of Puerto Rico, especially after they tried to assassinate President Truman at Blair House on 2 November 1950. Washington and London collaborated to remove the alleged communist Progressive People's Party of Cheddi Jagan, his wife, and Forbes Burnham from Parliamentary control in British Guiana, by suspending the constitution and intervening militarily. Today, Cheddi Jagan is back in power as President of the Cooperative Republic of Guyana, with the endorsement of Washington. In the English-speaking Caribbean, the "communistic" regime of Maurice Bishop in Grenada felt the ironfist of the Reagan Administration. The only survivor of this anti-Communism, Cold War campaign by the United States in the circum-Caribbean today is the regime of Fidel Castro, which came to power in Cuba in 1959. Of some interest, however, a report of 3 March 1958 by the Office of Naval Intelligence entitled "Communist Cold War Efforts in Mexico, Central America and Caribbean" said this about Fidel Castro: "There is no evidence of definite ties between the Communists and the current revolutionary movement led by Fidel Castro."

Other overlapping security/stabilization devices to the OAS and the ICBM-system in the post-1945 Caribbean region included the Caribbean Commission. Its members comprised Britain, France, the Netherlands, and the United States, the four then

Colonial Powers in the circum-Caribbean. The Caribbean Commission was formed in 1944–1945 out of an earlier 1942 Anglo-American body; and its stated mission was to advance "economic democracy" in the colonial possessions of the four powers. Paralleling the Caribbean Commission was the British effort to engineer a Federation of the British West Indies. In Central America, the countries experimented with a regional integration device.

By the 1960s, both the Caribbean Commission and the Federation of the West Indies were no more, and Cold War interstate differences in Central America that were fanned by Washington had pulled the steam out of the regional integration movement. The circum-Caribbean remained as before the arena of politics by the great powers, especially the United States.

This game continues to the present conjuncture, with the United States the dominant player. With the demise of the Federation of the British West Indies in 1962, the United States, with the collaboration of Britain, sponsored the entry of the independent Commonwealth Caribbean into the OAS. In the 1980s, the U.S. was also instrumental in organizing Barbados and her smaller English-speaking neighbors in the Leeward and Windward islands into a regional security system (RSS). The immediate raison d'être of the RSS was to counter the alleged security threat to these territories from the Communist regime in Grenada. Another raison, however, was to enhance their capability to deal with a new security threat to those countries and to the United States, namely narco-trafficking. With the demise of the Bishop regime and the return of Grenada to the RSS family, the focus is now on narco-diplomacy to deal with the security threats of narco-trafficking in the circum-Caribbean.

Lastly, the United States fashioned the Caribbean Basin Initiative in the 1980s, the rationale again being to stiffen the democracies in the circum-Caribbean in the continuing fight against residual Communism. More realistically, the CBI with its economic philosophy of enhancing the role of the private over the public sector in Caribbean "development" is a neocolonialism bag of the United States in the region. It is complementary and competitive to other neocolonial bags in the region, namely the European Union-African Caribbean and Pacific Group under the Lomé Conventions, or the EU-ACP; and CARIBCAN. The former represents the continuing neocolonial stake of the European Caribbean Colonial Powers, now members of the European Union; CARIBCAN is the expression of a continuing Canadian economic stake in the region, especially the English-speaking parts. The loser in all this is the within-regional integration movement of the Commonwealth Caribbean, in the form of, first, the Caribbean Free Trade Area (CARIFTA) and secondly, the Caribbean Community (CARICOM). The latter is currently engaged in efforts, via the establishment of the Association of Caribbean States (ACS) to bring in non-English-speaking countries in the circum-Caribbean.

The geopolitical reality of the circum-Caribbean today is one of continuing balkanization and domination by external powers. This is how the stronger external powers want it, and the strongest of them is the United States.[10] Geopolitical stratification, however, is linked with economic and social stratification in imperialism. Also a component of imperialism is cultural imperialism. The second part of the paper discusses some of these nexi in the century of U.S. domination of the circum-Caribbean.

THE SOCIAL NEXUS OF U.S.-CARIBBEAN RELATIONS

The United States and the countries embraced in our definition of "Caribbean" have been and are tied into a range of social relationships. Historico-sociologically, all shared the core experience of New World slavery. One result was a stratification that gave a monopoly of political, economic, and sociocultural power to European-diasporic groups over native Indians and imported Africans in the pre-Emancipation period. With this went a deepening of racism and ethnocentrism by the European stream: albeit deeper among the Anglo-Saxons than the Latins partly for sociocultural reasons.

In the structural adjustment that Emancipation brought in stages to the Americas, new labor factors were introduced from Europe and Asia mainly. One objective by the ruling élites was to provide competitive, cheap labor to the newly-freed African populations mainly. Relatedly, however, the objective—influenced by the scientific racism and eugenics of the nineteenth and twentieth centuries—was to promote "whitening" in the United States, Cuba,

Costa Rica, Argentina, and Uruguay, most successfully.[11] One thing was clear about Emancipation: It was never intended by its architects to alter the domination-subordination relationship that had developed between the North Atlantic tier and their peripheries in the circum-Caribbean and elsewhere in the Atlantic system of business. Secondly, the aim of Emancipation was to maintain, as far as possible, power and high status in circum-Caribbean and Latin American countries in the hands of white and neowhite social categories.

Today, changes have occurred. In the English-speaking Caribbean, blacks and Indians, descendants of slaves and indentures from Africa and Asia, hold political power. Economic power and high social status, however, still reside generally in what can be termed a pigmentocracy of whites, neo-whites, Chinese, Jews, and Syrian-Lebanese. In Jamaica, for example, a celebrated 21 families, with residency and citizenship rights in North America and Europe, dominate the local sectors of manufacturing, construction, and distribution that has developed since the end of World War II.[12]

In Trinidad and Tobago, the work of Camejo and Parris of the Social Sciences Faculty of The University of the West Indies has elucidated the existence of a local interlocking directorate of so-called "French Creoles" (of French, Spanish, and British descent), Chinese, and Syrian-Lebanese in banking, insurance and other sectors of business.[13] Barbados is commonly known as Little England, one reason being the continuing dominant role of the old slavery plantocracy in local business. In turn these interests in the English-speaking or Commonwealth Caribbean are interlocked with dominant interests in North America and Europe.

In the rest of the circum-Caribbean, mainly Hispanic and Catholic, social relations between the various categories may be freer.[14] Notwithstanding, there is a pigment line to political power, economic privileges, and social status—even in Marxist-Socialist Cuba.[15] In Haiti and the Francophone Caribbean, power, wealth, and social status separate a minority of Europe-descended and Europe-socialized whites, coloreds, and blacks from a mass of blacks.

As the United States, with its historically sharp white-black sociology, penetrated the circum-Caribbean in this century, one sociological result has been the reinforcing of the pigment line in circum-Caribbean countries. In Cuba, U.S. intervention worked to "roll-back" the advance of Afro-Cubans who had played an important role in the winning of independence from Spain. It also dispossessed Afro-Cubans from land in the eastern part of the island, for U.S. TNCs in agriculture and for the construction of the Guantanamo base. The local beneficiaries were the old Spanish/Cuban elites. The Afro-Cuban resentment over this process exploded in the "Guerra de Las Razas" in May-June 1912. It was crushed ruthlessly by a combination of U.S. and local Cuban military-security forces.[16]

U.S. expansionism into Haiti, the Dominican Republic, and Nicaragua before and after World War I was seen by Presidents "Big Stick" Roosevelt and Woodrow Wilson as bringing those states "into the twentieth century," with some validity in terms of contributions to modernization (health, roads, and infrastructure). Equally, modernization, including agriculture, resulted in land dispossession of the poorer people mainly; and the occupation or quasi-occupation enabled Americans to extend their racist attitudes into those countries. In Haiti, the occupation, symbolized in the 1916 decision to reinstitute forced labor or the corvee, provoked an Indigenous/Negritude movement known as the Haitian Renaissance.[17]

In the French and British Caribbean, as well as in the U.S. Virgin Islands, United States expansionism into World War II provoked fears among African leaders especially about the extension of Jim Crowism to their territories.[18] Data for the British Caribbean show that it also led to significant land acquisition for base construction during World War II under the 1940–1941 Destroyers-Bases Agreement. According to North Burn, the United States acquired from Britain a total of 87,000 acres of land in the base territories.[19] This is an underestimate, as the data in Table 2.1 show.

The acreage of land acquired by the United States was apparently greater than the table indicates. For example, the Governor of Antigua gave a figure of 1,700 acres for that colony—equivalent, he said, to almost 10 percent of the arable land.[20] The Trinidad data listed acquisition in Chaguaramas, site of the major wartime base, at the islands of Huevos, Chacachacare, and Monos only and not on the adjoining mainland. There are no data for the Bahamas. Though the bulk of the land leased or given by the British belonged

Table 2.1
U.S. Land Acquisition under the Destroyer-Bases Agreement

Territories	Total Acreage	Crown	Privately Owned
Newfoundland	18,268.000	15,467.000	2,801.000
Bermuda	1,427.000	1,040.000	387.000
Jamaica	24,383.767	16,050.846	8,332.921
Antigua	1,332.850	46.500	1,286.350
St. Lucia	2,730.230	141.000	2,589.230
Trinidad	23,061.950	10,319.660	2,742.290
British Guiana	17,636.240	14,879.780	2,756.460
Total	88,840.037	57,944.786	30.895.251

Source: Adapted from a document in RG59: Box 4677, folder #4: 811.34544/4–346.
Lt. John S. Gerety (War Dept. Gen. Staff) to Miss Borjes (Div. Br. Commonwealth Affairs, State Dept.), 3 April 1946. Also 811.34544/4–546, Navy Dept.
to Miss Borjes, 5 April 1946.

to the Crown, over 30,000 acres of private lands were lost to owners.
Both the British and the Americans cited appraisal value for the
lands, but the data were incomplete. The British figure tended to
be higher than that of the Americans. Only in respect of Newfoundland and Bermuda was there Anglo-American agreement on appraisal values: $1,416,525 or $506 per acre for the private lands in
Newfoundland; and $1,461,699 or $3,777 for those in Bermuda.
Those figures were credited as "reciprocal aid." Clearly, the two
powers were playing a statistical game at the expense of private
owners in the base territories. It is sociologically significant, however, that there was an agreement for Newfoundland and Bermuda. The private owners there were mainly British- and United
States-born whites who lobbied hard to protect their interests. By
contrast with Newfoundland and Bermuda, the other territories
with weaker concentrations of British and American whites regis-
tered considerably lower appraisals for acquired private lands:
$82.50, Antigua; $51.40, Trinidad (with the noted exception); $40.78,
St. Lucia; and $32.66, Jamaica.

Coming out of World War II, the United States, amid criticisms
by local officials and others,[21] handed back some of the Crown

lands mainly to colonial governments under so-called "Agricultural Utilization Agreements"—in Trinidad, St. Lucia, Antigua, and Jamaica. Guided, however, by the recommendations of a team headed by Senator James A. Mead that conducted an 8,000-mile inspection of the United States naval and air bases in the circum-Caribbean as well as in Ecuador between 25 March and 4 April 1945,[22] the "Agricultural Utilization Agreements" had clauses to permit repossession of the lands at 48 hours' notice "in the event of a war breaking out in which the United States is involved, or of any other overriding military necessity as determined by the Government of the United States of America"—as in St. Lucia in 1952.[23] Such language repeated the "military necessity" clauses in the Destroyers-Bases Agreement, as advised by the Mead Report.[24]

One "military necessity" reason for all this was that the United States was refitting the wartime bases in the Caribbean into their postwar ICBM system to counter the "Iron Curtain" bloc in the era of the Cold War, none more so than Trinidad and Bermuda. U.S. Joint Chiefs of Staff document 570/168 of 14 March 1951 read "Trinidad within the North Atlantic Ocean Region or NAOR"; a memorandum of Chief of Staff of the United States Air Force of 30 March 1954 addressed the reposition of Bermuda within a GLOBE-COM network of Receiver Stations of NATO.[25] In Trinidad, the continuing interlock of the wartime American bases into the NATO system was politicized by the rising nationalist movement of Eric Williams. The "Chaguaramas Question" entered domestic politics; the politics of the Federation of the British West Indies, when Chaguaramas was chosen as the site of federal capital; and international politics between 1958 and 1961.[26]

Complex negotiations between the United States, Britain, the Federal Government, and Trinidad (the latter two not yet legally independent) produced an agreement on "United States Defense Areas in the Federation of the West Indies" of 10 February 1961. Under it, the United States agreed to return 80 percent of all the lands it had acquired in 1940–1941 under a 99-year lease: 23,000 acres in Jamaica, 21,000 acres in Trinidad, and 900 acres in Antigua. The expiration of the original lease was changed from 2039 A.D. to 1977 A.D. Of some significance, however, the United States held on to the key "military necessity" sites, including Chaguaramas.[27]

The year 1977 has come and gone. There have been official statements that the United States no longer holds Chaguaramas. But many people, including me, are sceptical about such officialese. The sceptics include the families and other interests who lost their private lands in 1940–1941. Currently they are pressing the government of Trinidad and Tobago to return their lands—including taking legal action.[28] The lands in the area are under the administration of an authority, The Chaguaramas Development Authority. Controlled land-sea usage is the reality: In the word of the *Sunday Express* of Trinidad and Tobago of 24 March 1966, there is "little or no squatting" of lands, unlike the rest of the country; rather, there is "a public golf course, nature trails, historical sites, some bathing facilities, an agricultural project, and within the last few years a thriving yachting industry has developed."[29]

THE "REAL ESTATE" OF CARIBBEAN TOURISM: THE U.S. STAKE

As the preceding articles show, base lands in Trinidad and Tobago are tied up in Caribbean Tourism. The same appears to be true elsewhere in the region. Where not true, North Atlantic-sponsored tourism in the circum-Caribbean, with its lovely beaches, and so on, has soaked up more land in a generally land-constrained environment. Entering Grenada in the wake of the U.S. rescue mission of 1983 against the Maurice Bishop regime, U.S. Secretary of State George Schultz described the island as "a lovely piece of real estate,"[30] that is, for tourism. This is the Schultz Corollary to the Monroe Doctrine, as "the neoplantation enterprise" of tourism exploded in the circum-Caribbean after 1945, reinforcing existing social stratification.

As Frank Taylor has shown, between 1919 and 1937, tourism in the islands of the Caribbean Basin had grown from 45,000 to 204,000 visitors. Toward the close of World War II, the Anglo-American Caribbean Commission, conducted a survey to assess the potential value of the Caribbean territories for tourism. The findings were published in 1945 as *The Caribbean Tourist Trade—A Regional Industry.*[31] The decades of the 1950s to the 1970s saw the establishment of the Caribbean Tourism Association and its research arm, the Caribbean Tourist Research Centre. These instruments brought together, under external promptings, the British, Dutch, and French territories as well as Cuba, the Dominican Republic, and Haiti to map a strategy to increase the region's share of an anticipated surge in international tourism after 1945, with the wider civilization of air transport.

By the 1980s, the results speak for themselves. To quote Clive Y. Thomas, "the industry soon came to be dominated by the TNCs, with 13 Holiday Inns, 9 Hiltons, 9 Sheratons, 8 Trust House Fortes, 7 Club Mediterranee de Paris and 6 Grand Metropolitan (Inter-continentals) operating in the region."[32]

Following a pattern set by Juan Trippe in 1945 who locked PAA into the International Hotel Corporation, Trans World Airways, United Airlines, Eastern, and American Airlines of the United States, as well as airlines of the European Colonial powers in the Caribbean, interlocked air travel with tourism development in the Caribbean by the 1980s. The pattern remains today. One of the main within-Caribbean airlines to face this external competition became British West Indian Airways (BWIA), started by Britain in World War II and taken over by an independent Trinidad and Tobago in 1962. Trinidad and Tobago's effort to make BWIA the regional airline of the Commonwealth Caribbean, with horizontal linkages to other non-English-speaking territories in the region and vertical linkages to the "colonial" metropoles, is a saga of Caribbean and international relations. The effort is currently in a state of limbo. In 1995 the Government of Trinidad and Tobago virtually delivered BWIA to a U.S. private group known as the Acker Group in a domestically-controversial "privatization." Why controversial? C. Edward Acker, one of the chief American negotiators of the "privatization" on behalf of U.S. interests such as Acker's own Atlantic Coast Airline, and the first Chief Executive Officer (CEO) of the new BWIA, Arcadian Partners, had a history of stripping airlines such as PAA. Faced with adverse public opinion in Trinidad and Tobago, the government, while taking a minority share portfolio of 34.5 percent in the new Acker Group BWIA, negotiated what is called a "Golden Share" veto power over certain eventualities. Under the "Golden Share," the government won a veto over the following:

- ANY MERGER or consolidation with, or sale of all or substantially all of BWIA's assets to, any person, including without limitation, any Caribbean air carrier.

- ANY voluntary liquidation or dissolution.

- ANY strategic alliance or joint venture with any Caribbean carrier.

- THE acquisition, sale, transfer, or relinquishment of any route authority or operating rights involving Trinidad and Tobago.

- ANY change in jurisdiction of incorporation, location of principal executive offices or any of the headquarter operations to a jurisdiction outside of Trinidad and Tobago, or any change in the name of new BWIA.

- APPOINTMENT, compensation, and dismissal of each of the chairman of the board, deputy chairman, CEO, chief financial officer, and of new BWIA or any other officer with similar responsibilities but with a different title.

- ANY transaction between new BWIA and any affiliate.

- ANY proposed amendment to the articles of association of new BWIA that alters or amends the rights and privileges associated with the Golden Share or the governance provision as set out in the Investment Agreement.

The government of Trinidad and Tobago, now controlled by a party that had opposed the deal with the Acker Group, has had to invoke its power under the"Golden Share," as a crisis broke in February-March 1996 over the new BWIA management. Acker, the CEO, and Edward Wegel, the new American President and Chief Operating Officer of BWIA, were fired by the Board. Pledging to bring in a U.S. $10.5 million profit and an operating cash flow (after all expenses) of U.S. $21 million in the first year, the new CEO landed BWIA instead with multi-million U.S. dollar losses, juicy US consultancy contracts for former airline colleagues, a U.S.$2,600-a-month BWIA administrative office in Washington about which (it) neglected to tell shareholders and the board of directors, and an upscale house on the pricey slopes of Lady Chancellor Road (in the hills over Port of Spain, the capital), close to former BWIA chairman-turned-director, Joe Esau.[33]

It is important to note that the demise of BWIA will benefit U.S. airlines which dominate air travel and tourism in the Caribbean. Was Acker the front man in a bigger United States airline conspiracy to subvert BWIA and to regain an earlier monopoly over the air traffic in and out of the Caribbean, with implications for the tourism industry? One does not know.

The reality is that the United States accounts for the largest percent of the tourism in the Caribbean. Between 1970 and 1985, the circum-Caribbean accounted consistently for 2.6 percent of global tourism: 3.24 of 168 million arrivals in 1970 and 8 of 325 million in 1985. Of those 8 million in 1985 the United States accounted for 66 percent, Canada for 6.5 percent, and Britain and Western Europe for 10.2 percent. The principal Caribbean destinations of U.S. tourists by 1985 were five territories: Puerto Rico and the U.S. Virgin Islands (United States Caribbean) and the Bahamas, Jamaica, and Bermuda (Commonwealth Caribbean). Dollarwise, visitor expenditures in Caribbean tourism in 1985 stood at over U.S. $5 billion. Of this figure, the "big five" accounted for about 50 percent. The growth has continued since.[34]

In devising their tourism-development thrust in the 1970s, Caribbean Governments, aided by the CTA and affiliates, calculated on winning a greater capture of badly-needed foreign exchange and an increase in employment in a high-unemployment and under-employment region. Neither has happened to the extent hoped for. For example, Barry, in a case study of the Bahamas, has shown that only 19 cents of every U.S. dollar in the tourism industry for this territory enters the domestic economy.[35] The industry has generated some domestic employment. But the employment stratification of the Caribbean tourism industry mirrors the race/color of the slave plantation. The "new slaves" include nattily-dressed, poorly-paid, and mainly black waiters, waitresses, taxi drivers and security guards. The down side also includes male and female prostitution. The beaches of the Caribbean are filled with macho, black "beach bums" who are ready to commoditize sex to white female tourists. They and others are also ready to commoditize other highs such as marijuana and cocaine.

NARCO-TRAFFICKING IN THE CARIBBEAN BASIN

In the circum-Caribbean, the graph of narco-trafficking has grown in tandem with the growth of tourism. This is not to suggest that tourism is the sole or principal cause of the growth of narco-trafficking in the circum-Caribbean in the past two decades. More fundamentally, the international drug trade, like tourism, is a function of the North Atlantic-dominated international economy. As Gilbert James puts it:

A commodity—narcotic drugs—abundantly produced in some poor economies, which desperately need foreign-exchange earnings are absolutely dependent on export production, finds its way into markets in affluent economies, rich in hard currencies and with an effective demand for large commodities of the commodity.[36]

The Caribbean place in the international narco-trade derives from its status as a producer of marijuana, one of the commodities. It is also proximate to a principal source of cocaine, another commodity. Marijuana is produced in significant amounts in Jamaica and Belize in the Commonwealth Caribbean. The world's largest producers of cocaine are in South America: Colombia and Bolivia, with Venezuela, Brazil, and Ecuador as smaller producers. Within this core, an estimated 271,600 metric tons of coca leaf were produced; providing a potential supply of 770–806 tons of cocaine.[37]

The other side for the nexus is the demand for both and other drugs in the United States. In the words of a 1988 report of the United States Congressional Research Service: "America is consuming drugs at an annual rate of more than six metric tons (mt) of heroin, 70–90 mt of cocaine, and 6,000–9,000 mt of marijuana—80 percent of which are imported." U.S. consumption of cocaine alone doubled by 1993, and the market value stood at U.S. $15-17 billion.[38]

Assets of rugged land and unguarded coasts render the land-sea region of the Caribbean Basin ideal for the transit of cocaine, especially to North America as well as to Western Europe. Add to this the markup of a kilogram of cocaine from U.S. $3,000 in South America to U.S. $6,500 in Trinidad, to US $20,000 in New York City, and to U.S. $40,000 in Western Europe, in the context of the adverse economic impact on Caribbean and Latin American societies of the structural adjustment of the International Monetary Fund in the 1980s[39]—and we have a good part of the explanation for the cancerous involvement of politicians, diplomats, businessmen, the judiciary, the police, the military, the customs et al. in the narco-trade in these countries. The logistics of the transportation of the narco-trade between South America and North America and within the Caribbean Basin include mules, aircraft, fishing boats, and sophisticated speedboats and yachts, a "new modeling" of the land-sea-convoy system of the circum-Caribbean during World War II.[40] Little and big people are involved, with the latter virtually untouchable on account of status. The architecture of the international narco-trade in the circum-Caribbean embraces money laundering via a plethora of banks in some of the tiniest islands in the Caribbean Basin: such as the British Cayman Islands and Anguilla, both non-independent.

The circum-Caribbean international narco-trade and its ramifications were the subject of a workshop organized by the University of the West Indies' Institute of International Relations, Trinidad, on 19–21 January 1995 in Trinidad. Papers presented included Maureen Crane-Scott's "The Impact of International Narco-Trafficking on the Domestic Structure of Commonwealth Caribbean States"; Ivelaw L. Griffith's "Drugs and Criminal Justice in the Caribbean"; Ralph Henry's "Narco-Trafficking in the Commonwealth Caribbean: Some Economic Issues"; Gilbert James's "The Appropriateness of International Drug Traffick Control Policies to Caribbean States: A Case for Small State Narcodiplomacy "; Charles H. Morley's "The Impact of Money Laundering on State Security"; Karl W. Munroe's "Surviving the Solution: The Extraterritoriality Reach of the United States"; Trevor Munroe's "Democracy and Drugs in the Caribbean"; Barry Rider's "Taking the Profit Out of Corruption"; Trinidad and Tobago Defence Force's Major Dave L. William's "The Intelligence Challenge to the Caribbean States in Response to International Narco-Trafficking"; and Tim Wren's "Multilateral Co-operation With Reference to Financial Crime and International Narco-Trafficking."[41]

Moreover, in late 1995 into 16–29 March 1996, *Caribbean Week*, published by Caribbean Communication Inc. in New York City, carried a five-part series on the latest narco-trafficking in the Caribbean. The U.S. *Time* of 26 February 1996 featured an article by Cathy Booth entitled "Caribbean Blizzard." The daily and weekly presses in Trinidad and Tobago are replete with news concerning the region's involvement in the international drug trade as evidenced by the following headlines in the *Sunday Guardian* of 31

March 1996, p. 4, "Panama police seize 1,575 pounds of cocaine," concerning the discovery of 700 kilos of cocaine hidden in a boat and the arrest of a Panamanian. The location of the cocaine was said to be "the Darien jungle near the Colombian border," a corridor that "is used by Colombian drug traffickers to hide clandestine processing laboratories from where cocaine is shipped to the United States"; "Colombia's president hails arrests of major drug lords," that is, the arrest of Luis Alfonso Maquilon Amaya and Juan Carlos Ortiz Escobar of Colombia's CALI cartel in the narco-trade to North America and Europe on 29 March; the gunning down of a third CALI kingpin, José Santacruz Londono on 5 March; on the action of Juan Carlos Ramirez Abadia, another CALI kingpin in turning himself in to the authorities on 15 March; and on the U.S. pressure on President Ernesto Samper, said to have taken money from the CALI to finance his successful 1994 campaign, to crack down on the country's drug lords. The United States' narco-diplomatic pressure on the Samper government included the 1 March decision "to decertify Colombia as a full-fledged partner in the global anti-drug fight." "DR outlaws money launderers" concerns the conclusion of a United States-Dominican Republic agreement to outlaw money-laundering, to eliminate bank secrecy, and to authorize drug raids on homes of suspected principals in the regional and international narco-traffic.

In a "new-modeling" of the convoy system of World War II between the United States and the Eastern Caribbean, with Puerto Rico as the Headquarters of the Caribbean Sea Frontier, the American Commonwealth is the "center of the Caribbean drug trade," with the uncomplimentary status of the "New Miami" in terms of its high rate of drug-related crime.

Trinidad and Tobago in the Commonwealth Caribbean is a key leg in the convoy of cocaine from Colombia via Puerto Rico and Mexico to the United States. It, too, has a frightening surge of drug-related crime that has earned the territory the title of "the Wild West."[42] One local magnate in prison awaiting trial has been linked with the systematic elimination of a number of State witnesses: one of them under the custody of the Trinidad and Tobago Defence Force in an experimental Witness Protection Scheme. The victim is said to have slipped his State protectors on the weekend of Carnival, the national festival, that is, 16–20 February. His bullet-ridden and partly-burned body was found in an abandoned car on the morning of 20 February, Carnival Tuesday!

It is developments such as these and the reported lodgment of some U.S. $463.7 billion,[43] part of it believed to be drug money, in the money-laundering haven of tiny British-administered Cayman Islands in the Caribbean Basin *alone* that have prompted a concerted counter narco-diplomacy by the United States, the European Community, and the G-7. In 1986 the U.S. Congress passed the Money Laundering Control Act that made it "a major felony to conduct transactions involving the proceeds of crime," including drug money. The instrument, progressively tightened in 1988, 1990, 1992, and 1994, was deployed by the U.S. Customs to bust the *BCCI*, said to have had connections with Saddam Hussein's Iraq. In 1989–1990 the European Community and the G-7 countries established the 40 guidelines of the Financial Action Task Force (FATF) for its members in the fight against the international narco-trade and money-laundering. Almost in parallel, the OAS and the Caribbean subsystem fashioned comparable regulations, under the influence of the FATF and of the Inter-American Drug Abuse Control Commission (CICAID). The latter regulations are called the OAS Model Regulations.[44]

One result of all this in the OAS and Caribbean subsystem is an on-going U.S. narco-diplomacy-offensive to enmesh the countries in a network of treaties to deal with the regional drug menace, including money-laundering. The offensive includes the deployment of the U.S. Drug Enforcement Agency (DEA) and U.S. military forces in OAS and Caribbean countries, as well as within their waters under international law, that is, extraterritoriality.

Warren Christopher, in the first visit to Trinidad and Tobago by a U.S. Secretary of State since that of Secretary Vance in 1977, signed three instruments with the government of Trinidad and Tobago on 4 March 1996. Signing for Trinidad and Tobago was the country's first elected Indo-Trinidadian Prime Minister, Basdeo Panday. The three instruments, said to be a first within the OAS-Caribbean nexus, are as follows:

1. An Extradition Treaty
2. A Mutual Legal Assistance Treaty
3. A Maritime Counter Drugs Operation Agreement

They bear the print of the FATF and OAS Model Regulations.

In immediate implementation of the third Agreement, Warren Christopher formally handed over to Prime Minister Panday four specialized counter-narcotics boats for the use of Trinidad and Tobago's Customs and Excise Division, in association with the U.S. DEA and other agencies, if necessary.[45] Indeed, the U.S. DEA has gone into action in a more public way than ever before in the fight against the local and regional-wide drug trade and related activities: on 22 March 1996 in a joint operation with units of the Trinidad and Tobago police force called the Crime Suppression Unit (CSU) and the Multi-Optional Police Section (MOPS). Simultaneously, military and police/security units and personnel of CARICOM and of the Regional Security System (RSS) conducted the 10th War Games in Caribbean waters, called "Tradewinds," in association with counterparts from the United States and Britain.[46] This is reflective of a new United States-led militarization of both the Commonwealth Caribbean and the wider Caribbean and Latin America, under the guise of the campaign against narco-trafficking and money-laundering. The new thrust is also threatening to Americanize the traditional Hispanic and British legal and judicial systems of these countries more and more.[47]

COMMODITIZATION OF THE U.S. WAY OF LIFE VIA CABLE TV AND OTHER INSTRUMENTS

Perhaps the greatest threat to societies and people of the circum-Caribbean today is the pervasive commoditization and consumption of the United States' way of life via cable television and other instruments. The process is long-standing in the American Caribbean, Haiti, Cuba, the Dominican Republic and in the Central American republics—coincident with the first phase of U.S. expansion from the late nineteenth century to 1939. In that period, it was spreading to British territories such as Bermuda, the Bahamas, and Jamaica and to Dutch Aruba and Curaçao. The process, however, engulfed the entire circum-Caribbean during World War II with the massive U.S. base-presence there. The growth in commoditization and consumption of things American was assisted by the U.S. personnel and the "social investments" of the bases. It was also helped by radio, the Hollywood film-cinema industry, and the wartime visits of noted Hollywood stars to entertain the forces.

In Trinidad and Tobago, for example, "psychic" benefits for locals from the wartime presence of the United States came to include the greater circulation of money (including the U.S. dollar), chiclets (chewing gum), and U.S. brand cigarettes. The Americanization of culture in wartime Trinidad and Tobago was also evident in calypsoes of the period; in the names adopted by steel bands such as "Casablanca," presumably to refer to the 1943 visit of President Franklin Roosevelt to Trinidad on his way home from (the) Casablanca (Morocco) with Churchill on the future direction of the war; or "Tokyo" highlighting the capital-target of Japan, the "enemy"; in carnival bands portraying U.S. marines and preferred by steel bands; and in tastes in films starring Roy Rogers and John Wayne.[48] Other socially-undesirable things were commoditized and consumed in the British colony, such as prostitution.

The massive commoditization of things American, however, has come with the post-1945 age of television and, more recently, of cable TV, the information revolution around computers, and now the Internet. The Americanization of the Caribbean way of life is further aided by the growth of Caribbean migration to the United States, of two-way air travel by families "at home" in the United States and in the Caribbean; by the growing air- and sea-transit package trade from Caribbean peoples in the United States to families "home"; and, lastly, by the greater opening-up of Caribbean and Latin American economies to the privatization ethos of the International Monetary Fund (IMF) and the World Bank, under programs of Structural Adjustment.

Television and radio stations in the circum-Caribbean, with a heavy dose of state control and ownership into the 1980s, are being "privatized" somewhat. With this development, U.S. TV TNCs such as ABC, CBS, and CNN are beamed daily into a growing number of homes in the region, including lower-income ones. The more affluent have dishes and cable TV, with more direct access to the consumption of programs on channels such as Discovery, Arts and Entertainment, E.S.P.N. International, Cartoon Network, and Cinemax. Finally, the fare includes Black and Hispanic stations, with CNN also having Spanish-language transmissions at certain periods of the day and night. Through this one medium of cable

TV is commoditized a wide range of things American, for consumption by people in the circum-Caribbean. They even commoditize the same 800 number used by people in the United States and dependencies for contacting the suppliers of the advertised goods and services of U.S. capitalism for an appropriate fee.

As students of modern comparative North Atlantic imperialism know, the troika of civilization, Christianity and commerce have marched hand in hand. Of these, the components of civilization and Christianity have represented perhaps the most violent aspects of cultural imperialism. Galtung described cultural imperialism in the imperial venture as "violence that attacks the soul" of the colonized,[49] while Martiniquan-born Frantz Fanon in his book, *Wretched of the Earth*, equated cultural imperialism with psychological violence aimed at destroying the identity and mind of the colonized.

Whether intended deliberately or not, U.S. cable TV is waging U.S. cultural imperialism on the minds of Caribbean peoples in the sense described by Galtung and Fanon. The image of the United States that it transmits is that of White America: with its culture of suburban supermarkets, fast food, and White Christianity. The culture of fast food embraces Kentucky Fried Chicken, McDonald's, Pizza Boys, Coca-Cola, and Pepsi, to name some. Today, these symbols of the American fast-food culture have physical presences in almost all circum-Caribbean countries as in India, Communist China, many African countries, and the old Communist Iron-Curtain countries in the post-Cold War, New World Order.

Likewise, the image of U.S. Judaeo-Christianity that enters Caribbean homes via TV is white, fundamentalist Protestant, segregated, and sometimes weird. The episode of WACO and the Branch Davidians, led by David Koresh, was seen in the Caribbean by shocked locals. WACO, however, was dress-rehearsed in the jungles of the Cooperative Republic of Guyana in the 1980s by the mass suicide of Jim Jones and his "Doomsday" community of believers. Cable TV also transmits news of the activities of other cults in the United States, some of them articulating notions of "Christian white supremacy" and the theology that blacks and non-whites are the Cursed of Ham-Canaan-Cain and even "mudmen" beyond the pale of humanity, also that Jews are "the children of Satan."[50]

Some of the U.S. Christian Churches that have entered the circum-Caribbean and Latin America have been associated with the above theology. One is the Mormon Church, now present in several countries of the Commonwealth Caribbean, with governments led by black politicians and with African-descended people forming a significant percent of their population. How come? Under the "freedom of worship" provisions of the constitutions of these countries, the Mormons could not be kept out, especially as they had announced that they had had a new "revelation" concerning the Curse-of-Ham-Canaan-Cain thing! Secondly, as oral data for Trinidad and Tobago show, the Mormons enlisted the service of a prominent black Caribbean civil servant and a Knight of the British Empire today to present their application for Incorporation by Act of Parliament to the government of Trinidad and Tobago. The distinguished presenter was advised that the Parliament of Trinidad and Tobago was unlikely to support such a modus of entry. Instead, a backdoor entry was recommended, namely that the Mormons register as a "company" under existing company laws. The advice was that the Mormons should then lie low and show a more public face after a while. That was done.[51] Today, the Mormons have a brand-new church building in Port of Spain, from where they send out missionaries to other territories.

Data supplied by a secret source in a key Ministry in Trinidad and Tobago show the number of "missionary licenses" issued by the government of Trinidad and Tobago in the past five years. I have been reliably informed that the bulk of them went to U.S. churches and missionaries:

Year	Number of Missionary Licenses
1991	262
1992	278
1993	222
1994	143
1995	109
1996	21
	(to end of March)

It would be instructive to get such data for the rest of the circum-Caribbean, say in the last two decades. The momentum of U.S.-style fundamentalist Protestant evangelism has been quickening in the Hispanic Caribbean and Latin America, except Cuba. This is causing concern to the Roman Catholic Church in the Vatican and in the region, as the new Protestant Churches erode their membership oft times by providing social-welfare programs to the populace. Every now and again, these evangelists engage in actions that reveal their socialization in the sharp white-black culture system of the United States. In Brazil, a white American Protestant evangelist desecrated a "Black Madonna" icon of the Roman Catholic Church there, provoking angry reaction by citizens of the country's "racial democracy."[52] What if he had gone into the confrádias and seen the veneration of the Virgin Mary and other Catholic Saints as orishas of the Yoruba-transferred Faith in Brazil?[53]

Of course, U.S. cable TV commoditizes "Afro-beat" and "Hispanic-beat" in the form of music, dance, and sports particularly. "Afro-beat" music is a changing blend of U.S. African-American, Afro-Caribbean/Latin, and Continental African forms across the African Diaspora, backed up with dance forms, hairstyles, dress, and hip walk-and-talk.[54] In sports, "Afro-beat" is displayed in the basketball of the National Basketball Association and other competitions in the United States, with their heroes, inter alia, Magic Johnson of the Los Angeles Lakers and Michael Jordan of the Chicago Bulls.

"Afro-beat" music, dance, and basketball performers boost African pride and consciousness in the Caribbean Basin. There are, however, some insidious sides to this type of commoditization of culture by the U.S. TV media,[55] and the videocassette industry in the case of music. Firstly, the projection advances the consumption of cassettes and the paraphernalia of the basketball industry (jerseys, caps, etc.). It is common in the Commonwealth Caribbean today and, no doubt, in other linguistic areas of the Caribbean, to see young people, not just of African-descent, wearing jerseys, etc., marked "Sixers" and "Bulls."

Next, the projection of U.S. basketball (also U.S. football and baseball), with a longer history in the non-English-speaking Caribbean, is threatening to undermine the British-derived sports of cricket and football in grass-roots society in the Commonwealth

Caribbean. Thirdly, the projection of these U.S. sports and the Afro-beat music, and so on, perpetuates a stereotype that blacks are good only at entertainment and sports. They may be good film-producers like Spike Lee and good Hollywood stars like Denzel Washington and Eddie Murphy but not good enough for Oscars. Finally, the much-publicized news of Magic Johnson's HIV-positive affliction or the rape-charge and imprisonment of Mike Tyson, U.S. black boxing star, compounds an historical erotica in the Western culture that black males are oversexed and animalistic.

U.S. TV transmitted the specter, confidence-boosting to Afro-Caribbean, of the Black Power movement in the United States as part of the civil rights movement. The heroes were West Indian-linked Stokeley Carmichael and Malcolm X. The latter was connected to the Nation of Islam, the African-American black Muslim organization. Today, its leader is part West Indian-descended Louis Farrakhan. Both Malcolm X and Farrakhan are heroes in the eyes of many young Afro-West Indians, as evidenced by the public wearing of jerseys, etc. Branches of the Nation of Islam exist in Commonwealth Caribbean countries such as Trinidad and Tobago today: before the Farrakhan-sponsored and TV-transmitted "Million Man March" of Afro-descended males in the United States in late 1995. Here again, however, U.S. TV beams a subtle or non-so-subtle message to white-dominated United States and to the racially- and ethnically-divided Caribbean that Black Power poses a threat to system stability. In Trinidad and Tobago, this threat materialized in the 1970 Black Power Revolution, including an attempted coup d'etat by "black" officers of the new Trinidad and Tobago Defence Force; and, in 1990, in another attempted coup d'etat by the Jamaat al Muslimeen, a Black Muslim organization under the leadership of Yasin Abu Bakr, an ex-policeman in the local Police Force. In both instances, the government of Trinidad and Tobago had to call on the United States for military and other assistance in order to suppress the insurrections and to maintain system stability.[56]

CARIBBEAN MIGRATION TO A "CARIBBEANIZATION" IN THE UNITED STATES

There are two sides to a "social nexus." So far, I have focused on the United States' side of the nexus in terms of the impact of U.S.

imperialism on the "plural" societies of the circum-Caribbean. Generally, U.S. imperialism has been operating in system maintenance and system reinforcement of the "pigmentic" social stratification that was shaped by slavery—even where, as in the Commonwealth Caribbean, blacks and Indians have come to political power.

There is, however, a second side to the nexus of U.S.-Caribbean relations, especially since World War II: the growth of Caribbean migration, legal and illegal, to the United States and their sociocultural impacts, in different degrees, on life in that country.

Caribbean migration into the United States is long-standing. The streams have included and continue to include Hispanic, Francophone, Dutch, and Anglophone. From Brazil, considered by some to be Caribbean on historico-sociological grounds on account of slavery, comes a Portuguese-speaking stream. The U.S. Immigration and Naturalization Service (INS) has not differentiated these streams in any scientific way for a long time. Accordingly, statistics of legal Caribbean immigration to the United States are at best proximate, even to the present. One compilation by the INS for the period between 1820 and 1988 is shown in Table 2.2.

The data show the rise of Caribbean immigration to the United States between the end of the U.S. Civil War and the passage in 1921 and 1924 of the eugenics-influenced Quota Acts, to tilt immigration into the United States in favor of the Anglo-Saxon/Nordic stream of Europeans and against "lesser" Europeans, Asiatics, and blacks, including those in the Caribbean. The impact of these measures show up in the sharp drop in the figures for the Caribbean between 1921 and 1940. The graph began to move back up during and after World War II as, for example, the plural United States began recruiting Anglo-Caribbeans, especially for farm work in the United States. The great surge came with the passage of the McCarran-Walter Act of 1952 and the further liberalization of measures in the 1960s. The tide of legals included "political refugees" from circum-Caribbean countries, such as the Dominican Republic and Cuba in the Cold War—mainly fair-skinned Hispanics. In contrast, the pigmentic bias in INS policy for Caribbean immigration was manifest in their categorization of the black Haitian exodus from Haiti in the post-Duvalier, post-War era as "economic refugees" and not "political refugees."[57]

Table 2.2
Caribbean Immigration to the United States, 1820–1988

Period	Number of Immigrants	Period	Number of Immigrants
1821–1830	3,834	1911–1920	123,424
1831–1840	12,301	1921–1930	74,899
1841–1850	13,528	1931–1940	15,502
1851–1860	10,660	1941–1950	49,725
1861–1870	9,046	1951–1960	123,091
1871–1880	13,957	1961–1970	470,213
1881–1890	29,042	1971–1980	741,126
1891–1990	33,066	1981–1988	671,819
1901–1910	107,548		

Sources: Adapted from U.S. Immigration and Naturalization Service (1989, Table 2, pp. 2–4): in the essay "Caribbean Exodus and the World System," by Alan B. Simmons and Jean Pierre Guengant, Chapter 6, pp. 94–114 (data at p. 95), in Mary M. Kritz, Lin Lean Lim, and Hania Zlotnik (eds.), *International Migration Systems: A Global Approach* (Oxford: Clarendon Press, 1992).

Of course, there is an indeterminate flow of illegal immigration from the circum-Caribbean into the United States, especially from Mexico and across the United States-Mexico long border. Estimates run into the millions. The Hispanic illegals, however, include Dominicans in large numbers, who get into the United States via Mexico and Puerto Rico. According to Hobart A. Spalding, some 2.5 million illegals from the Dominican Republic "solicitaron la amnistad bajo el programa de legalización" of the INS in 1988.[58] This illegal surge from the Caribbean is part of a wider surge of non-white immigration into the United States in recent decades. It is threatening to change the existing demographics of the country, politicizing the immigration issue as in 1900–1920. The Hispanic flow into Florida-to-California has heightened fears of Hispanization of this subregion of the United States: evidenced in Proposition 197 of the Republican-controlled state government of California to cut off schooling and health care for the mainly Mexican or Chicano stream into that state. Or, there is the call by former Senator Robert Dole, Republican candidate for President in the U.S. elections in

November 1996, for English to be made the official language of the United States, an issue in state politics in Florida, with its heavy Cuba/Hispanic migrant population. History, however, is full of cruel ironies. The Hispanic immigration into the Florida-to-California line can be described as "colonization by reverse," in that this area formed part of the Spanish (also Franco) Empire in the Americas and was acquired by the United States by purchase and conquest, mainly at the expense of Mexico in the pre-Civil War period.

Be that as it may, the Hispanic flow into the United States is having its sociocultural and other impacts on areas such as Florida, California, and New York-New Jersey. They bring their Roman Catholicism, taking over many an abandoned church or sharing Mass in Spanish in some churches, with Mass in English for non-Spanish-speaking Catholics. They bring their high birth rate, too—to the concern of the Malthusians. Finally, they bring their Hispanic beat in the form of Hispanic TV and radio stations in some locales; Hispanic newspapers; and Hispanic/Latino music and dance. The meeting between Hispanics from different countries of the Caribbean, the Hemisphere, and Spain is contributing to a certain internationalization of Hispanization in the United States. Simultaneously, there is a growing Spanish/American bilingualism via the contact with Americans and other English-speaking communities, in areas such as New York and New Jersey.

The Haitians and the mainly Afro-West Indians from the Commonwealth Caribbean also bring their flavor to urban settings in the Atlantic states from New York to Florida. For example, Haitians and Afro-Trinidadians bring their Vodun and the Orisha religious expressions, along with their Judaeo-Christian Catholicism and Protestantism. In places such as New York, such Afro-based religious expressions meet with the Santería and the Candomblé of Afro-Cuba and Afro-Brazil.[59] In turn, all are reinforced by contact with Continental Africans from Nigeria and the Republic of Benin, where these expressions originated. In areas of high concentration of Haitians and Afro-West Indians, such as New York City and adjoining cities in New Jersey, radio stations such as WLIB beam community and "home" Caribbean news, music, etc; there are also newspapers and food stores that cater to their needs. Interestingly, in Newark and adjoining areas in New Jersey, the author has observed that the food stores with Caribbean and Continental West

African food items are owned by Koreans, many of whom appear to speak little English, much less French patois.

With specific reference to the Commonwealth Caribbean migrant communities in the East Coast, we note the diffusion of their reggae (Jamaica) and their Carnival and steelpan music (Trinidad and Tobago). Jamaica reggae and other music forms have become "world beat" in the United States and in many G-7 countries. The concept of "world beat" is usually linked with Western/North Atlantic musicology.[60]

According to Rawle Gibbons, Director of the Creative Arts Centre of the University of the West Indies, St. Augustine, Trinidad, the street festival of Carnival "is growing fastest in Europe and North America, claiming in these countries over 100 cities." The European cities include Notting Hill in London, venue of perhaps the biggest Carnival in Britain and the European Union. In the United States and Canada, there are annual Carnivals in Brooklyn, New York City; Miami, Florida; Atlanta, Georgia; Toronto; Ottawa; and Montreal. These overseas Carnivals are serviced by the Carnival industry in Trinidad and Tobago and the wider Commonwealth Caribbean, including bands, calypsonians, and so on. The service agencies include steel bands.

The steelpan was declared the National Instrument of Trinidad and Tobago in 1994. Starting in the 1970s, the Faculty of Engineering of the University of the West Indies and the Caribbean Industrial and Research Institute (CARIRI) in Trinidad conducted tests, with a view to developing the mass production of steelpans for the domestic and international market. Some results have been achieved. A pressing bowl has been developed for mass production of "pan." In 1992 a set of standards for the instrument was published. Ohio in the United States, however, appears to be ahead of the local Trinidad and Tobago industry in mass-production of steelpans. There, a company known as "Pan Yard Inc." is "having an extraordinary production capacity of pans and its accessories." "Pan Yard Inc." works in conjunction with the University of Akron, Ohio, which offers a steel band course within its pedagogy. The first such course was introduced in 1973 at the University of Northern Illinois. By contrast, the University of the West Indies, Trinidad, introduced courses in steelpan music for undergraduates only in the late 1980s.[61] The preceding index some of the Caribbeanization of culture and of pedagogy in the United States, related to the greater presence of Caribbean-originating peoples in that country. The pedagogical changes are reflected, for example, in growing Caribbean studies and/or Hispanic studies at universities in the United States.

Entering into the United States are the so-called "dot" people, that is, Indians from the Indian sub-continent and the Indian diaspora in Africa and the Caribbean.[62] The largest concentration of Indo-Caribbeans in the region are in Suriname; the Cooperative Republic of Guyana; and Trinidad and Tobago. Their rise in politics in the circum-Caribbean is demonstrated by the fact that the last two Commonwealth Caribbean countries now have elected Indo-Caribbeans as their heads of government: Cheddi Jagan, Executive President of the Cooperative Republic of Guyana, and Basdeo Panday, Prime Minister of Trinidad and Tobago. Additionally, the constitutional President of Trinidad and Tobago is an Indo-Trinidadian of the Muslim Faith, against the Hinduism of the Prime Minister.

I have no data relating to the number of Indo-Caribbeans in the United States. Generally, more of them tend to migrate to Canada, partly on account of the role of the Canadian Presbyterian Church in missionary education to those communities in Trinidad and Tobago and in ex-British Guiana in the era of indenture. The Canadian exodus, however, includes Hindus and Muslims. Quite conceivably, the U.S. exodus includes Indo-Caribbeans of Christian, Hindu, and Muslim adherence. The Hinduism and the Islam of these migrants from Suriname, Guyana, and Trinidad and Tobago must interact with each other in the United States, also with the Hinduism and Islam of migrants from the Indian sub-continent (India and Pakistan) and, in the case of Islam, North Africa, the Middle East, and Indonesia. With what results within the culture-mix inside of the United States, or with what feedback into the ethnic politics of the three Caribbean countries? We cannot say. With what effect on United States policy toward the Caribbean? Also we cannot say. For certain, the Indo-Caribbean dimension is much more a part of the "social nexus" of U.S.-Caribbean relations than before; so, too, the Hispanic dimension, with the formation of the Association of Caribbean States.

CONCLUSION

I have covered much ground in this paper on the social nexus of United States-Caribbean relations, especially from World War II to the present. Even so, I am conscious of the fact that I have not touched on several aspects. For example, how the Cuban-American nexus in Florida continues to affect U.S. foreign policy, as evidenced by the recent shooting-down by the Castro regime of aircraft of the exile group, Brothers to the Rescue, said to be shunting food and other supplies to kith and kin in Communist Cuba but really bent on destablilizing the regime. The reaction of the Clinton Administration and of the Republican-controlled Congress is well-known: the passage of an embargo measure with clear extraterritorial ramifications for Canada, the European Union, and the CARICOM states, among others.[63] Next, there is the intriguing question of how the intellectual property provisions of the Uruguay Round would affect the social and other nexus of relations between the circum-Caribbean and the United States.[64] Colleagues in the Department of Economics at the university campus in Trinidad tell me that the United States would be the gainer in the nexus of intellectual property, thereby deepening the existing unequal relationship with the circum-Caribbean.

NOTES

1. Leslie Manigat, "The Year 1975 in Perspective (From the late 1950s to 1975: The Emergence of the Caribbean on the International Scene)," in Leslie F. Manigat (ed.), *1975: The Caribbean Yearbook of International Relations.* Leyden: A.W. Sijthoff, with the Institute of International Relations, The University of the West Indies (UWI), Trinidad & Tobago, 1976, pp. 55–137.

2. The discussion on this is based on the author's UWI, Ph.D. thesis (1983) entitled "The European Possessions in the Caribbean during World War II: Dimensions of Conflict and Cooperation," 2 vols., 1072 pp.

3. For the concepts "The American (U.S.) Lake," "Quarter-sphere" Defense" and "Hemisphere Defense," see John Child "From 'Color' to 'Rainbow': U.S. Strategic Planning for Latin America, 1919–1945," *Journal of Inter-American Studies & World Affairs* (J.I.A.S. & W.A.), 21 #2, 1979 and "Strategic Concepts of Latin America: An Update," *Inter-American Economic Affairs*, 34, 1980.

4. Baptiste, vol. 2 of thesis, p. 1033 and n. 33, p. 1041 for General Board of the Navy's document: 414–3: 780, 24 January 1918, "Ownership of Islands and Reefs Pending in Pacific and Elsewhere." Also G.B. 414–3: 753, 6 August, 1917: "Sovereignty and Control over Certain Islands and Harbours in Caribbean and Panama."

5. Baptiste, vol. 2 of thesis, p. 1033 and n. 24, p. 1040 for G.B. document.

6. G.B. 404, 20 March, 1919: Chief of Naval Operations to General Board, Naval War College and Bureau of Docks, with enclosure. Also R.G. 80, Box 39: P.D. 126–1.

7. Baptiste, "The Exploitation of Caribbean Bauxite and Petroleum, 1914–1945," *Social and Economic Studies*, 37 #1–2, March–June, 1988 (B.W. Higham ed. Special Issue: Caribbean Economic History), pp. 107–142.

8. Baptiste, *War, Cooperation and Conflict: The European Possessions in the Caribbean, 1939–1945*, Westport, CT: Greenwood Press, 1988.

9. Baptiste, "Caribbean Decolonisation caught between the Manchester Principles and the Cold War:" presentation at the Conference, "Africa in the World: The 1945 Pan-African Congress and its Aftermath," Manchester Town Hall, Manchester, England, 13–15 Oct., 1995 (under the partial sponsorship of Manchester University's Department of History). 45 pp., (quote at p. 15). This paper is to be published in the proceedings of the conference.

10. For recent publications of Caribbean international relations, see, in Warwick University Caribbean Studies, Paul Sutton (ed.), *Europe and the Caribbean* (1991) and Anthony P. Maingot, *The United States and the Caribbean* (1994), MacMillan Caribbean.

11. The literature on this is growing. See Daniel J. Kevles, *In the Name of Eugenics*; Vernon Briggs, Jr., *Immigration Policy and the American Labor Force*; Donald K. Pickens, *Eugenics and the Progressives*; and Robert A. Divine, *American Immigration Policy*, 1924–1952 (United States). On Eugenics in Germany, see Robert Jay Lifton, *The Nazi Doctors: Medical Killing and the Psychology of Genocide*. Thomas E. Skidmore's *Black and White: Race and Nationality in Brazilian Thought* throws light on this subject in Brazil and, by inference, in Latin America. Also Abdias Do Nascimento, *Brazil: Mixture or Massacre? Essays in the Genocide of A Black People.*

12. Clive Y. Thomas, *The Poor and the Powerless: Economic Policy and Change in the Caribbean*, New York: Monthly Review Press, 1988, p. 190.

13. Acton Camejo, "Racial Discrimination in Employment in the Private Sector in Trinidad & Tobago," *Social and Economic Studies*, 20 #3, September 1971, pp. 294–318; and Carl Parris, "Power and Privilege in Trinidad & Tobago," Ibid., 34 #2, 1981, pp. 97–109. Also, Selwyn Ryan and Taimoon Stewart (eds.), *Entrepreneurship in the Caribbean: Culture, Structure, Conjuncture*, Institute of Social and Economic Research (ISER), UWI, St.

Augustine, Trinidad, (printed by the Multimedia Production Centre, Faculty of Education), 1994.

14. Lloyd King, "Cultural Perceptions in the Relations between the Caribbean and Venezuela," *Caribbean Affairs* (Special Spanish/English language issue: *Simón Bolívar, El Libertador: Venezuela en la Unificación del Caribe*), July 1994, pp. 58–73.

15. Carlos Moore, *Castro, the Blacks and Africa*, Los Angeles: Center for Afro-American Studies, University of California, 1988.

16. Luis A. Pérez, Jr., "Politics, Peasants and People of Color: The 1912 'Race War' in Cuba Reconsidered," *Hispanic American Historical Review*, 66 #3, pp. 509–39.

17. There are several good studies on Haiti under the US Occupation (1915–1934), including by David Healy; R. Logan, Ludwell Lee Montague; and David Nicholls.

18. Baptiste, Ph.D. thesis, vol. 1, pp. 180, 183–84.

19. North Burn, "United States Base Rights in the British West Indies, 1940–1962," Ph.D. thesis, Fletcher School of Law and Diplomacy, 1964, p. 60.

20. R.G. 59:811. 34544/10–1749, Box 4682, folder #4: Br. Embassy Note #516, 17 October, 1949 to State Dept.

21. For criticisms by Grenada's Theophilus A. Marryshow and other leaders at the 1945 West Indian Labour Conference, see R.G. 59:811. 34544/10–1945,/Box 4677, folder #1/Whitaker, (US Consul, Grenada) to State Dept. #345, 19 October, 1945, with enclosure from the local newspaper, *The West Indian* of 26 September, 1945.

22. Same series: 34544/3–2445, Box 4675, folder #2, Note dd. 24 March, 1945 from Capt. John H. Kennedy (Navy) to State Dept. (departure of the mission on 25 March); and paper 7/2645: Box 4676, folder 6, Frank Merkling, Asst. Sec., State to DC/R (Filing), 20 July, 1945: "Tentative Report on Caribbean Inspection Trip" with letter dd. 26 July by Mead, Chairman of the Special Senate Committee Investigating the National Defense and Chief Counsel to the Committee.

23. Burn, op. cit., p. 64.

24. Baptiste, Ph.D. thesis, vol. 1, Chapter 8, esp. pp. 399–430.

25. In author's article cited at n. 9, p. 16.

26. Burn, pp. 97–158; and Carl Parris, "Chaguaramas Revisited" in *1975: The Caribbean Yearbook of International Relations*, op. cit., pp. 254–83.

27. Burn, p. 146.

28. See Anthony Milne, "Chaguaramas: The Real Story," Section 2, *Sunday Express*, pp. 1–4; and same issue, Section 1, "Focus on Chag: Claims of former owners dismissed in court," pp. 14–16. According to the latter, Justice Margot Warner, in an hour-long judgement issued in the Hall of

Justice, Port of Spain on 24 January, 1994, threw out a constitutional motion in the name of families who lived in Chaguaramas before 1941. She ruled that the lands were acquired "out and out" by the Crown in 1941 under the provisions of the *Land Acquisitions Ordinances, 1925 to 1941*. The families have appealed the ruling and the matter is still to come before the Court of Appeals in Trinidad and Tobago.

29. Anthony Milne's article, "Maqueripe breathes again," *Sunday Express*, Section 2, 24 March, 1996, pp. 2–3. Gail Alexander, writing on "Scotland Bay in dispute" in the *Sunday Guardian* of the same date at p. 21 noted that the lands in dispute are valued at over $3 billion TT, i.e. US $500,000 at the current exchange rate in Trinidad and Tobago.

30. Quoted at p. 122 of Gordon K. Lewis, *Grenada: The Jewel Despoiled*, Baltimore and London, John Hopkins University Press, 1987 & 2nd printing in 1988.

31. Frank F. Taylor, *To Hell with Paradise: A History of the Jamaican Tourist Industry*, Pittsburgh and London: University of Pittsburgh Press, 1993, p. 165. For his description of Caribbean tourism as "neoplantation enterprise," see p. 175.

32. Clive Y. Thomas, op. cit., p. 147.

33. Camini Marajh, "Govt. bids for new control: As BWIA picks up the pieces at the demise for the Acker-Wegel regime," *Sunday Express*, 3 March, 1996, p. 19. The journalist gave the following break-down of the shareholders in the "Acker-privatised BWIA": Government of Trinidad and Tobago, 34.5 percent; C. Edward Acker, 0.5 percent; Employees and Bargaining unions representing BWIA workers, 15.1 percent; Gordon Cain, Chairman of Arcadian Partners and a Director of Acker's US-based airline, Atlantic Coast, 9 percent; Roytrin (local bank), 7 percent; Unit Trust of Trinidad and Tobago and a para-Statal, 5 percent; Lant & Co., 7 percent; Loeb Partners, 3 percent; Edward Wegel, .5 percent; Mike Stanfield, acting BWIA CEO, 0.7 percent; and Joe Esau, BWIA Chairman who participated in the privatisation negotiations, and was member of the new Acker BWIA and chairman of Allied Caterers Ltd., which was interlocked as caterers to BWIA, 0.1 percent. See also Vernon Khelawan, "Quo Vadis BWIA?," *Sunday Guardian*, 3 March, 1996, p. 17; and David Nanton, "Board in the dark over Acker spending," *Trinidad Guardian* (Business Section), 6 March, 1996, p. 4.

34. Clive Y. Thomas, op. cit. pp. 150–58. inclusive of various tables.

35. Ibid., p. 161.

36. For reference, see papers of the conference on "The Impact of International Narco-Trafficking on the Security of Caribbean States," listed at p. 29. The quote in James' paper is at p. 12.

37. James, p. 8.

38. Ibid., p. 11. See, too, Anthony Maingot, *The United States and the Caribbean*, chapter 7, "Threats to Social and National Security: the Internationalization of Corruption and violence," pp. 142–62 and chapter 8, "The 'offshore' development strategy: Is it for everyone?," pp. 163–82.

39. As quoted in article in issue of the *US Time* of 26 February, 1996, p. 28: see p. 29 and n. 42.

40. For the land-sea convoy in the Battle of the Caribbean of 1942–3 against Hitler's U-boats, see the author's, *War, Cooperation and Conflict* (1988).

41. See n. 36 for theme of the Workshop.

42. *US Time*, 26 February, 1996, p. 26 (Puerto Rico) and p. 28 (Trinidad). The terms are attributed to the respective US DEA agents covering the Caribbean territories.

43. Cited in section about the Dominican Republic in the *Sunday Guardian*, 31 March, 1996, p. 4, in main body of the paper. See also Ivelaw Griffith's fine coverage of the Caribbean money-laundering havens in his conference paper read at the Narco-Trafficking Conference in Trinidad, pp. 8–14; and the series in *Caribbean Week*.

44. For this, see papers presented by Charles H. Morley and Tim Wren at the Narco-Trafficking Conference in Trinidad.

45. *Trinidad Guardian*, 5 March, 1996, p. 1. Secretary Christopher noted that Trinidad and Tobago had placed itself in "an unusual category" by signing all three agreements. Inter alia, he promised United States' assistance to Trinidad and Tobago and the CARICOM in the establishment of a Witness Protection Programme. For other coverage of Christopher's visit to Trinidad and Tobago, which was cut short on account of the Hamas-engineered "suicide bombing" in Tel Aviv, Israel on Sunday, 3 March, 1996, see Gail Alexander, *Sunday Guardian*, 3 March, 1996 "State visitor: First visit since 1977" and a profile of the career of the US Secretary of State; p. 16; and *Trinidad Guardian*, 4 March, 1996, p. 1: airport arrival ceremony, in which Christopher described Trinidad and Tobago "as a magnet for foreign investment." Also the coverage in the two other dailies, *Newsday* and the *Express*, including their Sunday issues of 3 March, 1996.

46. For this, see Francis Joseph, "Give up, DEA tells suspect," *Trinidad Guardian*, 25 March, 1996, p. 1; and same newspaper, 22 March, 1996, p. 10 (re: "Tradewinds"). Just prior to Secretary Christopher's visit, the US DEA and the same Trinidad and Tobago units conducted an anti-marijuana cultivation operation.

47. Alma H. Young and Dion E. Phillips (eds.), *Militarization in the Non-Hispanic Caribbean*, Boulder, CO: Lynne Rienne Publishers, 1986.

48. Quoted from author's unpublished paper, "The Presence and Impact of the United States in the Caribbean during World War II, with Special Reference to Trinidad," delivered at a USIA-sponsored seminar on the *United States Presence in the Caribbean*, 1783–1962," Carapachima Senior Comprehensive School, 13 February, 1987, p. 14. See also his "Colonial Government, Americans and Employment generation in Trinidad, 1939–1945," (Unpublished Paper, UWI, Trinidad, 6 December, 1985).

49. Galtung, "Violence, Peace and Peace Research," *Journal of Peace Research*, 3, 1969, pp. 167–71.

50. The same view is held by a number of US white-supremacist militia groups such as The Freemen. See also William Edwards, "Scientific Racism: Persistence and Change," *Trotter Review*, 2 #3, (Fall), 1988.

51. Oral interview with the Government Minister at the time, Sunday, 7 April, 1996. To preserve confidentiality, the author has chosen not to mention the name of the Minister, his Ministry and the name of the Caribbean personality who acted on behalf of the Mormons. It is this ex-ministerial source who told the author of "missionary licences" that are issued by the Government of Trinidad and Tobago annually; and directed him on sourcing such data.

52. The author witnessed the episode on a CNN newscast a month or so ago.

53. This theme is covered in the author's course in *African Diaspora II* (1800 to the Present), taught to Final Year students at his Trinidad Campus of the University of the West Indies. The first part of the course examines the evolution of negative somatic-norm-imaging of blackness from the late Classical Period into the era of the trans-Atlantic in the cultures of Judaeo-Christianity, Islam and Hinduism.

54. For insights on this process, see foreword, "On the Black Diaspora and its Study" in Aubrey W. Bonnett and G. Llewellyn Watson (eds.), *Emerging Perspectives on the Black Diaspora*, Lanham, Maryland, University Press of America, Inc., 1990, xvii. See also article in n. 60.

55. See, for example, "Racial Stereotyping: The Role of the Media," papers presented at a forum at the William Trotter Institute, University of Massachusetts at Boston, 26 February, 1990, 30 pp. Also Kirk A. Johnson, "Media Images and Racial Stereotyping," *Trotter Review*, 1 #2, (Summer) 1987 and other articles in that issue. The theme pervades succeeding issues of the *Trotter Review*.

56. Selwyn Ryan, *The Muslimeen Grab for Power: Race, Religion and Revolution in Trinidad and Tobago*, Port of Spain, Trinidad: Imprint Caribbean Ltd., 35–37. Independence Square, 1991; and Selwyn Ryan and Taimoon Stewart (eds.), with assistance from Roy McCree, ISER, UWI, St. Augustine, Trinidad, 1995.

57. See, for example Jake C. Miller, *The Plight of Haitian Refugees*, New York: Praeger, 1984.

58. Hobart A. Spalding, "Los imigrantes dominicanos in Nueva York," *El Caribe Contemporáneo* (Mexico), 19 (July–Dec.), 1989, pp. 63–80, 78.

59. On the antecendents of Vodun in New Orleans back to the late 18th century, see Jessie Gaston Mulira, "The Case of Voodoo in New Orleans," in Joseph E. Holloway (ed.), *Africanisms in American Culture*, Bloomington and Indianapolis, Indiana University Press, 1991, pp. 34–68. The same book has a an essay by George Brandon entitled "Sacrificial Practices in Santería, an African-Cuban Religion in the United States," pp. 119–47. See also Joseph M. Murphy, *Santería: An African Religion in America*, Boston, Beacon Press, 1988. Finally, the Caribbean community in Boston was the subject of a conference in March 1996, organized by the Black Studies Program of Boston under Dr. Frank Taylor (Director). The theme of the presence of African-based religions in Boston was discussed (telephone conversation with Dr. Taylor, formerly on the staff of the History Dept., UWI, Trinidad).

60. Deborah Pacini Hernandez, "The Internationalization of Afrobeat / the Location of World Beat: the Picó Phenomenon in Cartagena, Colombia," paper read at the conference, "The World the Diaspora Makes: Social Science and the Reinvention of Africa," Ann Arbor, Michigan, 3–7 June, 1992, 36 pp. The conference was partly sponsored by the US Social Science Research Council.

61. Rawle Gibbons, "Pan in Focus" (Feature Address delivered at the Heritage Library, Knowles Street, Port of Spain, Trinidad, 21 February, 1996) and published in *Trinidad and Tobago Review*, (organ of the Trinidad and Tobago Institute of the West Indies, 24 Abercromby Street, Port of Spain, Trinidad and Tobago), 18 #1–3 (Easter) 1996, pp. 1 and 25. Also Sean Nero, "Pan continues to grow abroad," *Trinidad Guardian*, 15 March, 1996, p. 17.

62. For essays on this subject, see Mahin Gosine, *The East Indian Odyssey: Dilemmas of a Migrant People*, New York, Windsor Press, 1994. See, especially, Part V "Asian East Indians in the United States," pp. 165–95; and Part VI "Caribbean East Indians in the United States," pp. 196–222. The author wishes to thank Dr. Ken Parmasad, his colleague in the History Dept., UWI, Trinidad, for bringing this work to his attention and for loaning him his personal copy to consult.

63. Kevin Fedarko, "This Cold War Is Back," inclusive with an interview between Fidel Castro and Time representatives, US Time, 11 March, 1996. For CARICOM-Canada criticism of the Helms-Burton measure that seeks to push non-US companies for trading with and investing in Cuba, see Michael Becker, "Caricom, Canada not Bowing: Cuba 'Is Part of the

Region,' " *Caribbean Week*, 7 #12, March, 16–29, 1996, pp. 1–2. The criticism is contained in a communique of 5 March, 1996 at the end of a two-day summit in Grenada between Jean Chretien, Canada's Prime Minister, and CARICOM leaders (except Hubert Ingraham of the Bahamas and Ronald Venetian of Surinam). The communique expressed "strongest objection to the extra-territorial provisions of the bill which seeks to apply US domestic law to other countries." The Canada-CARICOM summit coincided with the narco-diplomacy-visit of the US Secretary of State, Warren Christopher, to Trinidad and Tobago. For his reaction to the Canada-CARICOM statement about the Helms-Burton measure, see p. 2 of article in *Caribbean Week*. The controversial bill has since been enacted by the US Congress and signed into law by President Clinton.

   64. Carlos A. Primo Braga, "Trade-Related Intellectual Property Issues: The Uruguay Round Agreement and its Economic Implications" in Will Martin and L. Alan Winters (eds.), *The Uruguay Round and the Developing Economies*, World Bank Discussion Papers #307, Washington, DC, The World Bank, October 1995, pp. 381–411; and Taimoon Stewart, *The Emerging Legislative and Regulatory Framework Governing Trade-Related Environment Issues: Implications for CARICOM Countries*, Institute of Social and Economic Research, University of the West Indies, St. Augustine, Trinidad, Jan. 1996. Again, the author acknowledges the help of a colleague in his Campus' Dept. of Economics, Dr. Shelton Nicholls, both for the documents and for sharing with him views on this aspect.

3

Economic Development of the English-Speaking Caribbean and Relations with the United States: Tourism and Migration

Jay R. Mandle

INTRODUCTION

On the eve of World War II, wrote Gordon K. Lewis, the English-speaking West Indies "were a decadent backwater, neglected by the British and overlooked by the Americans." American liberal opinion, he continued, had "been so concentrated on India that it had paid little attention, by comparison, to the British colonial debris on its own Caribbean doorstep" (Lewis 1968, 93). World War II brought an end to this disinterest, with the construction of military bases in the region, particularly the large ones in Guyana and Trinidad. American involvement intensified during the 1960s. U.S. corporations invested heavily in the region's bauxite and petroleum industries, with the result that as early as the 1960s the United States already was the region's most important trading partner (Palmer 1990, 1). But the involvement of the United States in the politics of the region, with isolated exceptions such as its opposition to Cheddi Jagan and his People Progressive Party in Guyana, awaited the end of British colonial rule, a process completed in the early 1980s. Now with the British all but absent, there is widespread agreement that, in the words of Bonham C. Richardson, "All Car-

ibbean societies, on the basis of location alone, remain geopoliti-
cally dominated by the United States" (Richardson 1992, 184).

Since the 1960s, the interaction between the West Indies and the
United States has been dominated neither by conventional economic flows—trade, capital, and aid—nor by overt U.S. political
involvement. Rather what is most salient in the relationship is the
movement of people. On one hand, millions of U.S. citizens have
visited the countries of the West Indies as tourists. On the other
hand, a substantial fraction of the population of the West Indies has
moved to the United States to reside. These population flows have
created a relationship that has influenced each side more than is
typically the result of conventional bilateral relations. One of these
influences—the impact on the economic development of the West
Indies—is the issue addressed in this paper.

TOURISM

Income growth in the United States and advances in transportation technology, largely developed in the United States, were
responsible for the growth of the tourist industry in the Caribbean.
A large tourist industry in the West Indies required household
incomes in the United States to reach sufficiently high levels to
generate an extensive demand for tropical vacations. After such a
level was reached, tourism possessed a high income elasticity of
demand. Increases in income resulted in disproportionately large
increases in consumption. But in addition to the expansion of
demand associated with U.S. income growth, the Caribbean tourist
industry, to reach its potential, also required the development of
high-speed air travel. With the emergence of the commercial air
travel industry, the cost and time spent travelling to the West Indies
was substantially reduced, further stimulating demand. Thus, as
Frank Fonda Taylor writes, "It was not until December 1930, when
Pan American World Airways first linked Jamaica with the outside
world via its Clipper service, that Jamaica began to emerge as a
leading destination for the average middle-income vacationer"
(Taylor 1993, 156).

Tourism grew rapidly during the post-World War II years, particularly in Jamaica, Barbados, and Antigua. Data on tourist arrivals in the early years are spotty. But by 1968, annual tourist arrivals

in the region totaled in excess of 600,000; 43 percent went to Jamaica, and about 20 percent journeyed to Barbados (Chernick 1978, 464). By 1987, Antigua and Barbuda, Barbados, St. Kitts and Nevis, and St. Lucia were all greeting more visitors per year than their own population size (Mandle 1996, 135). In 1993, tourist arrivals reached 2.3 million, a number that represents more than one-half the combined population size of the nations of the region. As in the early years, Jamaica was host to more than 40 percent of tourist arrivals, while Barbados's share had declined only slightly to about 17 percent (Caribbean Tourism Organization 1994, 5).

Throughout these years citizens from the United States dominated Caribbean tourism. Americans represented 55.4 percent of the tourists who came to the West Indies in 1968, a statistic that changed very little over the years, peaking at 56.5 percent in 1986 and standing at 52.4 in 1993. What this means is that in the single year, 1993, well over 1 million Americans came to the West Indies (Chernick 1978, 464; Caribbean Tourism Organization 1994, 55).

MIGRATION

While U.S. citizens were flocking to the West Indies to vacation, a reverse flow of people was getting under way. Starting in the 1960s, West Indies people for the first time moved, in large numbers relative to the population size at home, to the United States in search of a place to live. The triggering mechanism for this surge of emigrants was the passage of new legislation in Great Britain and the United States. During the late 1940s and 1950s, Great Britain had been the principal non-Caribbean country of destination for migrants from the West Indies. In the United States, during these years, the McCarran-Walter Act had all but prohibited the immigration of residents of colonies to it. But on both sides of the Atlantic, new legislation reversed the roles of the two countries. The 1962 British Commonwealth Immigrants Act effectively barred new arrivals from the English-speaking Caribbean. But the 1965 amendments to the McCarran-Walter Act drastically enlarged the opportunity for Caribbean people to come to the United States. Whereas previously the colonies of the region had been permitted to send only 100 migrants per year to the United States, under the new legislation, all locations in the Western Hemisphere, no matter their constitutional status, could share in the quota of 120,000 migrants (Kraly 1987, 39). In this new legal context, the flow of people from the Caribbean to Great Britain was all but terminated. That to the United States, though not large compared to other sources of migration, nevertheless was substantial when compared to the size of the home population (North and Whitehead 1991, 20).

Reliable data on this flow of population are scarce. However, recent World Bank estimates suggest that from 1980 to 1988 alone, the Caribbean annually lost almost 1 percent of its population to the United States. About one-half of this migration came from Jamaica, and another one-fifth came from Guyana. The region's highest rates of migration were experienced in St. Kitts where almost 10,000 people left this country of about 44,000, and Antigua, where 14.5 percent of the population left the island. The cumulative result of this migratory flow was that 727,191 people born in the English-speaking Caribbean were resident in the United States in 1990. This statistic represents 14.2 percent of the West Indies population of 5.1 million (Mandle 1996; 168, 174). To put this in perspective, if 14.2 percent of the United States citizens lived abroad, the total would come to just under 37 million people.

CONSEQUENCES OF POPULATION FLOWS

These population flows necessarily had a greater impact on the West Indies than on the United States. The roughly 700,000 West Indians in the United States are dwarfed by the 260 million people living in that country. But just the opposite is the case with regard to tourist arrivals in the West Indies. It is true that visitors to the Caribbean spend little time there, certainly in comparison to the length of time West Indians spend in the United States.[2] Nevertheless, to the extent that visitors influence the host society and economy, clearly the West Indies is more likely to be changed as a result of these population movements than is the United States.

There are two ways to argue that the West Indies benefits from this traffic in people. In the first place, the demand for tourism permitted the region to put to productive use its natural factor endowments—salubrious climate, gentle surf, and attractive beaches. If ever there was a region possessed of a comparative advantage, the West Indies does so in tourism. Not surprisingly, the tourist industry has been successful. As indicated in Table 3.1, restaurants and hotels, the categories that capture most but not all of the industry, make very substantial contributions to the gross domestic product in Antigua and Barbuda, Barbados, St. Kitts and Nevis, and St. Lucia, with Grenada not lagging very far behind. The industry too has been responsible for considerable employment growth (see Table 3.1). Thus there is no doubt that U.S. visitors are, in large part, responsible for tourism's emergence in the West Indies as a leading economic sector.

The second positive contribution concerns the safety valve that emigration may have provided. An argument to this effect is made by Averille White among others. White is skeptical that the region suffers because of the skills lost in the migration. She insists that "one must be realistic and the question to be considered is whether

Table 3.1
Percentage Contribution of Tourist Related Sectors to Gross Domestic Product and Tourist Employment as Percentage of Total Population, 1993

Country	Restaurants and Hotels as Percent of GDP	Tourist Employment as Percent of Population
Antigua	13.7	6.2
Barbados	13.1	NA
Dominica	2.3*	0.6
Grenada	7.6*	1.3
Jamaica	2.2*	0.9
St. Kitts	10.1**	2.7
St. Lucia	10.4	2.4
St. Vincent	2.6	NA
Trinidad	1.4	0.1

* 1992
** hotels only
$r^2 = 0.703533$, statistically significant at the 0.05 confidence level.

Sources: Adapted from Caribbean Tourism Organization, *Caribbean Tourism Statistical Report, 1993 Edition*, (Barbados: Caribbean Tourism Organization, 1994), Table 39, p. 93 and Table 51, p. 189.

employment and production would have been realised in the islands if the emigration outlet had not become available." Implicitly answering this question in the negative, White concludes that "it is quite likely that the level of unemployment in the islands might be even higher were it not for this 'safety valve' " (White 1987, 12).

But despite the fact that the two-way movement of people helped to spawn the tourist industry and provided employment options for mobile Caribbean people, it is nevertheless likely that the flow of population between the United States and the Caribbean produced a net negative impact on the West Indies' ability to achieve economic development. The process of modern economic growth is one in which technological advance, productivity growth, and the emergence of new sectors of economic activity become routine. There is not much doubt that this has not occurred in the region. The small size of the nations of the Commonwealth Caribbean means that their economic modernization will have to take the form of export promotion. Unlike many East Asian countries, however, the West Indies has not been successful in innovating in overseas markets (Mandle 1996).

Fundamental here is the weakness of the educational system in the region. It is simply inconceivable that a society can participate successfully in the modern world of technology with a poorly educated population. And yet poorly educated is the only way to characterize the West Indies people. A study by the World Bank gives content to this characterization. It reports that though virtually all children in ten West Indies countries complete primary school, a dramatic fall-off in all countries except Barbados and St. Kitts occurs between that level and entry into secondary school. Whereas in Barbados and St. Kitts over 90 percent of children enter secondary school, in the eight other countries that proportion is much lower, ranging from a high of 53 percent in Jamaica to 23 percent in St. Lucia. But the situation is even worse with regard to the completion of secondary school. Incomplete data, particularly the absence of data from Barbados in this regard, may produce a downward bias to the pattern. But the picture nevertheless is bleak. Of the five countries for which data are available, the probability of completing secondary school is highest in Jamaica at only 53 percent, and ranges downward in the other countries: 38 percent in Grenada, 26 percent in Guyana, and 21 percent in both St. Lucia and Belize. If the objective of the education system is to allow students to participate successfully in the modern world economy, it is unmistakably clear that it is failing in the West Indies. The World Bank itself concludes, "Until the primary schools can significantly improve the performance level of their graduates, and secondary schools and tertiary institutions offer a sound education for a much larger proportion of the age group than is currently the case, it is unlikely that most Caribbean nations' labor force will be capable of supporting a development strategy dependent more on human than natural resources" (World Bank 1993, 44, 45).

Though many share in the responsibility for this educational debacle, the relationship with the United States looms large in this regard. For that relationship has acted both to constrain the region's incentive to invest educationally in its children and at the same time to raise the price of doing so. On the one hand, tourist dominance has meant that there has been no strong pressure from employers in the region to improve the educational system. With the exception only of top managerial positions, tourist employment does not require the skills associated with modern technology. As a result, the leading economic sector in the region has not been a source of pressure on the region's schools to increase the supply of technologically competent personnel. In the absence of such pressure, the educational system has been free to drift. On the other hand, the migration to the United States has significantly raised the cost of improving the technical competence of the West Indies labor force. Well-educated workers are more than twice as likely to be present among emigrants than among the population resident in the region. As a result of this loss, it is necessary in the West Indies to invest in many more students than there will be additions to the supply of well-educated labor force participants. That means that even at the current low levels of educational attainment, in the words of the World Bank, "many countries are not reaping the full benefits of their social investment in education" (World Bank 1993, 12).

There are no specifically identifiable villains to blame for the fact that the West Indies' relationship with the United States has militated against economic development in the Caribbean. The relationship that has evolved is almost entirely market driven. A high degree of economic integration exists between the two regions in the tourist and labor markets. The outcome in each is what market theory would anticipate: a two-way traffic in people. The fact that these flows undermine hopes for economic development in the West Indies is entirely an unintended consequence of rational market behavior.

The clear inference to be drawn is that economic development will not occur in the West Indies simply as a by-product of the free-functioning of markets. Modern economic growth has its own requisites, particularly with regard to the supply of well-educated people. In a setting where market forces do not generate substantial stocks of human capital, a society is left with only two choices. It may accept the market outcome and be content to be an observer, but not a participant, in the process of economic modernization. Alternatively, it could consider this to be a case of market failure and purposefully intervene to create a more positive dynamic than markets produce. What is clear, however, is that this is a dilemma that confronts the West Indies and is rooted deeply in its relationship with the United States.

NOTES

1. An obvious exception to this is the United States' hostility to the People's Revolutionary Government in Grenada and its ultimate use of military force in that country in 1983.

2. According to the Caribbean Travel Organization, the length of stay of tourists ranges from 11.2 days in Barbados to 7.2 days in Grenada (Caribbean Tourism Organization 1994, Table 35, p. 84)

REFERENCES

Caribbean Tourism Organization. 1994. *Caribbean Tourism Statistical Report: 1993 Edition*. Barbados: Caribbean Tourism Organization.

Chernick, Sidney E. 1978. *The Commonwealth Caribbean: The Integration Experience*. Baltimore: The Johns Hopkins University Press.

Kraly, Ellen Percy. 1987. "U.S. Immigration Policy and the Immigrant Populations of New York." In Nancy Foner, ed., *New Immigrants in New York*. New York: Columbia University Press.

Lewis, Gordon K. 1968. *The Growth of the Modern West Indies*. New York: Monthly Review Press.

Mandle, Jay R. 1996. *Persistent Underdevelopment: Change and Economic Modernization in the West Indies.* New York: Gordon and Breach.

North, David S., and Judy A. Whitehead. 1991. "Policy Recommendations for Improving the Utilization of Emigrant Resources in Eastern Caribbean Nations." In Anthony P. Maingot, ed., *Small Country Development and International Labor Flows.* Boulder: Westview Press.

Palmer, Ransford W. 1990. *In Search of a Better Life: Perspectives on Migration from the Caribbean.* New York: Praeger.

Richardson, Bonham C. 1992. *The Caribbean in the Wider World, 1492–1992: A Regional Geography.* New York: Cambridge University Press.

Taylor, Frank Fonda. 1993. *To Hell with Paradise: A History of the Jamaican Tourist Industry.* Pittsburgh: University of Pittsburgh Press.

White, Averille. 1987. "Eastern Caribbean Migrants in the USA: A Demographic Profile." *Bulletin of Eastern Caribbean Affairs* 13, no.4.

The World Bank. 1993. *Caribbean Region: Access, Quality and Efficiency in Education.* Washington, DC: The World Bank.

4

In Search of a Better Life: Caribbean Migration to America

Ransford W. Palmer

INTRODUCTION

Even though history has separated the Caribbean into different language groups, population movement, investment flows, and trade constitute powerful links that tie the region to North America. Anything that alters these links alters fundamental U.S.-Caribbean relations.

The characteristics of population movements between countries tell us a great deal about the economic status of these countries. Nowhere is this better illustrated than in the movement of peoples between the United States and the Caribbean. A largely tourist population from the United States moves regularly to the Caribbean, and a population of immigrants, students, and temporary visitors move regularly to the United States. Aside from Mexico, these population flows are the largest between the United States and the developing countries of the Western Hemisphere. In 1990, the non-U.S. islands of the Caribbean received roughly 12 million visitors, most of them from the United States (Gayle and Goodrich 1993) and sent 83,300 permanent immigrants to the United States (Statistics Division, INS 1994).

THE DETERMINANTS OF MIGRATION

The principal determinant of these flows is the higher standard of living in the United States. On the one hand, the higher standard of living in America makes travel by Americans in great numbers to the Caribbean possible. On the other hand, Caribbean immigrants aspire to achieve the higher standard of living of the American tourist. Economists call this the demonstration effect. But this effect is also demonstrated by returning immigrants and by those who remit funds to relatives back home. Even if the returning immigrant is not truly successful, he or she usually displays the appearance of success, and money remitted back home brings with it the message that things are better over there.

The relationship between living standards and migration may be illustrated by a comparison of the experience of Trinidad and Tobago with that of Jamaica, Barbados, Haiti, and the Dominican Republic during the period 1966 to 1975 when the exchange rates were stable. As Trinidad prospered from the oil boom of the 1970s, Trinidadians traveled regularly in large numbers on their national airline to the United States for vacation and shopping. As a result of this, the ratio of temporary visitors (tourists) to immigrants from Trinidad to the United States, allowing for differences in transportation cost, was higher than that of the other four countries (Table 4.1). In general, the data for these countries show an inverse relationship between the per capita GDP and the share of immigrants in the total population movement to the United States. This phenomenon is easily observed in the movement of people between the United States and such developed countries as Canada, Western Europe, and Japan.

Other factors affecting migration include the stock of Caribbean immigrants in America and the family reunification feature of U.S. immigration policy. The large concentration of Caribbean immigrants in certain areas provides a familiar cultural environment for new immigrants. This concentration is reinforced by the family reunification policy which gives preference to close relatives of immigrants who are U.S. citizens.

Table 4.1
Ratio of Immigrants to Temporary Visitors from the Caribbean and Per Capita GDP of Sending Countries, 1966–1975

Country (US$)	Ratio	Per Capita GDP*
Barbados	1:11.7	814
Dominican Republic	1:4.2	438
Haiti	1:3.4	109
Jamaica	1:6.4	825
Trinidad & Tobago	1:10.5	1,086

* Average for the 10-year period, 1966–1975.

Sources: Adapted from Ransford W. Palmer, *Pilgrims from the Sun.* New York: Twayne Publishers, 1995; International Monetary Fund, *International Financial Statistics Yearbook, 1992.* Washington, D.C., 1992.

SETTLEMENT AND TRANSFORMATION

The relative economic success of West Indians in America has been documented by Thomas Sowell (1975) in *Race and Economics,* and in my own work, *Pilgrims from the Sun: West Indian Migration to America* (Palmer 1995). Data from the 1990 U.S. Census show (Table 4.2) that their median household income was equal to or greater than that for the population of the United States.

It could be argued, of course, that this success derives largely from the fact that migration tends to select the most resourceful people and that most of these immigrants settle in high-wage urban areas. But this explanation is too simple because it ignores the major obstacles faced by new immigrants as they are transformed from majority status in their home country into minority status in their new land. European immigrants, despite their many ethnic groups, did not go through the same kind of transformation since they became part of the white majority. How the Caribbean immigrant handles this transformation is critical to his or her success in a society with a long history of racism. The fact is that their transformation is never complete. Their memory of their majority status is kept alive by the many social and political organizations that interface with their countries of origin and by frequent visits back home. West Indian immigrants are among the most frequent flyers back to their home

Table 4.2
Median Household Income of the United States Population and West Indian Immigrants, 1990

Country	Median Income (US$)
Jamaica	30,461
Barbados	33,480
Guyana	33,904
Trinidad & Tobago	30,305
United States	30,056

Source: U. S. Bureau of the Census, *Profiles of Our Ancestry: Selected Characteristics by Ancestry Group, 1990.* CPH-L-149, Washington, D.C., 1990.

countries. This constant keeping in touch is a source of their psychological well-being as they cope with the problems of settlement in America. A clear manifestation of the incompleteness of this transformation is the unusually large share of them who have chosen not to become U.S. citizens, preferring instead to maintain their permanent residence status and to hold on to their old passport. (Over the last two years, however, new proposals in the U.S. Congress to limit public benefits for legal aliens have increased the rate of application for citizenship). A recent story in *The New York Times* of two settled middle-class Jamaican neighborhoods in the Bronx provides a powerful example of incomplete transformation. *The New York Times* reported a discussion with one family whose children attributed their success to "their sense of Jamaicanness." Nossiter 1995, B2), a sense that allows them to focus on the primary reason they chose to become immigrants, that is, the improvement of the economic well-being of their household, without being overly distracted by issues of race in America.

THE DOMESTIC ECONOMY OF THE COUNTRIES OF ORIGIN

On the surface, the opposing flows of tourists and immigrants may seem unrelated, like two strangers in an airport. Yet it is not unreasonable to argue that they are related in an indirect sense. For most Caribbean countries, tourism is the most important industry, providing employment for large numbers of people and foreign exchange and tax revenues for the national economy. Its comparative advantage resides in the balmy climate, excellent beaches, and proximity to the United States. Unfortunately the local economies are unable to supply a large share of the demand for goods and services that the industry generates. Hence imports create a persistent hemorrhage of the gains from the industry. This has severely limited the role of the industry as an engine of growth and development. The upshot is that the foreign tastes and preferences of the industry have had a far more powerful effect on Caribbean imports than on domestic production. Furthermore, the industry has done more to reinforce the perception that things are better over there than anything else that flows from North America. Against this background, it is therefore not unreasonable to view the flow of immigrants as a reflection of the unfulfilled potential of the tourist industry—an industry that is itself the manifestation of the good life but yet unable to create enough opportunities for a better life for those who are influenced by this manifestation.

It is undeniable that greater employment and production at home would allow the region to export more goods with labor embodied in it instead of exporting labor itself. This was an important objective of U.S. policy in the 1980s under the Caribbean Basin Initiative (CBI). Then it was argued that a greater flow of U.S. investment into the Caribbean would create employment and reduce the propensity of Caribbean people to migrate to the United States legally and illegally. Unfortunately the passage of time has not validated this argument.

Yet the role of U.S. investment as an indirect determinant of migration has an important place in the history of post-Emancipation Caribbean. In the early part of this century, U.S. investment attracted large numbers of West Indian workers to build the Panama Canal and to build railroads for the sugar and banana plantations of the United Fruit Company in Costa Rica and Cuba.

THE MOBILITY OF CAPITAL AND LABOR

The Caribbean remains a region with a surplus of labor and a shortage of capital. The surplus labor keeps wage rates low, and the shortage of capital keeps interest rates high. Neoclassical economic theory argues that if there are no obstacles to the mobility of labor and capital, labor would tend to move out of the Caribbean to seek higher wages elsewhere and capital would tend to move in to take advantage of higher rates of return. This rough pattern does exist even though the international mobility of labor is restricted by the immigration policies of destination countries. These counter movements of labor and capital would eventually arrive at an equilibrium situation where the disparity in international wages and interest rates would disappear. This would come about as foreign capital from the United States creates jobs in the Caribbean and raises wages. This would in turn reduce the desire of Caribbean people to migrate to the United States. This outcome may never be achieved, however, for three principal reasons. The first is that most of the U.S. capital investment in the Caribbean over the past twenty years has gone into labor-intensive assembly industries where wage rates are typically low. The second is the precipitous decline in Caribbean exchange rates, which has widened the wage gap between the United States and the Caribbean. The Jamaican dollar, for example, which was worth 16 U.S. cents in 1991 is now worth less than 3 cents. And the third is that a large share of those who migrate were not in the labor force. More about this group later.

The widening of the wage gap encourages further migration, a phenomenon that suggests that migration generates its own momentum. The widening wage gap is a reflection of the anemic performance of Caribbean economies over the past twenty years. Indeed, living standards in most of these countries today are no higher than they were in the early 1970s in spite of the appearance of modernization.

DISTRIBUTION OF INCOME AND OUTPUT

To the extent that immigrants displace native-born workers and cause wage rates to fall, migration may alter the distribution of income in America. Here it is important to note that immigrants do not always displace native-born workers. Many create jobs for themselves and for native-born workers; others take low-wage jobs that native-born workers refuse to take. The combination of low-wage immigrant labor with native-owned capital will increase profits and therefore change the distribution of income in favor of the recipients of profit. If the rise in profits offsets the loss in the wages of displaced workers, total national income will rise, supporting the argument that immigrants contribute to a net increase in the national wealth. If no workers are displaced, the increase in the national wealth would be even larger.

The availability of low-wage immigrant labor may also influence the composition of output by inducing the production of labor-intensive goods and services. In Kings County, New York, where the largest concentration of West Indians in America lives and where nurses and other medical technicians constitute a disproportionate share of the skilled and semiskilled immigrant work force, the delivery of health services is the major industry, with hospitals being the major employers. Here the causal relationship between the growth of this industry and the supply of immigrants is circular. In the first place, the supply of these immigrants is a response to the demand for them. As the industry grows, it further increases its demand for low wage-workers.

The growth of the health delivery industry in Kings County, New York, is typical of the growth of the urban service sector in America where a disproportionate share of low-wage jobs is created. This has led to greater inequality in the distribution of income in America today. Gary Burtless, an economist at the Brookings Institution, and Timothy Smeeding, a professor of public policy at Syracuse University's Maxwell School, point out that since 1973, "Families and workers at the top of the economic ladder have enjoyed rising incomes. Families in the middle have seen their incomes stagnate or slip. Young families and workers at the bottom have suffered the equivalent of a Great Depression" (Burtless and Smeeding 1995, p. C3). They show that the "hourly wages of workers with average or below average skills continue to slide," while "at the same time the percent of U.S. income received by the top 5 percent of households continues to climb, reaching new postwar highs almost every year" (p. C3). This has allowed them to conclude that "the rising tide is now lifting the yachts and swamping the rowboats" (p. C3). Social critics have long seized upon this growing inequality as a source of pessimism in America, arguing that today's children are not likely to do as well as their parents. If this is true, it would bring to an end the post-World War

II experience of upward mobility that has become second nature to American families.

Despite the actual or perceived trend toward greater income inequality, immigrants come in large numbers because they see a different kind of inequality. They see an inequality between their current economic status and the prosperity they perceive in America. They see the ability of the U.S. economy to create jobs at wages higher than they have ever earned as a powerful source of optimism about the future of their children. And so when they come to America, they contribute not only to the nation's output of goods and services but also to the revitalization of traditional American optimism. This immigrant optimism is reflected in what has become the overarching feature of contemporary migration to America—the migration of entire households for settlement.

MIGRATION OF HOUSEHOLDS

As households migrate, their internal dynamic is affected. Quite often, the migration of the Caribbean household is spearheaded by the woman because of the greater availability of job opportunities in the urban service sector for women immigrants. Some of these opportunities are created by the movement of native-born women into the labor force as well as by their movement away from some traditional occupations. The demand for nannies and nurses is the result of this process, and it has made these immigrants the care givers of America.

The household migration process itself may span several years. If there are children, they are usually left behind in care of relatives. After the migrating parent has found a job, he or she will remit funds back home to help finance the eventual reunification of the household. The flow of remittances in this context reflects the incompleteness of the migration process. As members of the household are reunited, the flow of remittances may taper off, with smaller amounts going to the extended family left behind.

Most of the women immigrants from the Caribbean are included in the largest group of immigrants classified as "housewives and dependents." Because this group was not recorded as part of the labor force in their home countries, their migration has had no direct effect on measured output and unemployment there. However, when these "housewives" migrate, they invariably seek employment, which allows them to contribute to the family budget for the first time. This new economic status may or may not bode well for harmony in the traditional Caribbean household, where the man has always seen himself as the sole provider. In some instances, the woman's new economic status may cause the family to disintegrate, especially when she migrates first and is joined after an extended period by the husband. In this situation, family reunification facilitated by U.S. immigration policy may be undone by the improved economic status of the woman immigrant.

Peter Brimelow (1995) has been critical of family reunification as an objective of immigration policy, arguing that "the immigrant would achieve the truest reunification if he returned home" and that " 'family reunification' permits immigrants after their arrival, to acquire and import foreign spouses, forming new families that never existed to be 'disunited' in the first place." Though undoubtedly some examples of abuse of the system can be found, immigration policy cannot view migration simply as a movement of individual workers. To the extent that each worker is part of a family unit, immigration policy is obligated to facilitate the reunification of that family.

For most Caribbean countries, the flow of foreign exchange in the form of remittances sent back by immigrants is second only to that generated by the tourist industry. For the Caribbean, remittances from immigrants represent the returns on past migration, whereas tourist spending is the result of current flows of tourists. Migration may then be viewed as a kind of investment, the cost to the home country being the resources allocated to educating and training the migrants before their departure and the future output of goods and services lost upon departure.

RECENT CONCERNS ABOUT IMMIGRATION

The concentration of immigrants in certain areas of the United States has raised concerns by state and local politicians about the ability of their economies to absorb the immigrants. This is essentially an argument about the ability of immigrants to pay taxes to finance the public services they consume. One recent study commissioned by the Carrying Capacity Network, a group that is lobbying for a moratorium on legal migration, estimates that there is a revenue deficit of $2,343 per immigrant (Huddle 1995). This estimate is grossly overstated because the study includes refugees and asylees among its population of 16.5 million immigrants. Further, it tells us nothing about the value of the additional output created by the immigrant work force, the increase in the profitability of the business firms using low-wage immigrant labor, and the future increase in output that will result from public investment in the education and training of the children of immigrants.

It may be argued that the problem of immigration is more one of local absorption than of national absorption, given the fact that the immigrants tend to concentrate in a handful of states. The problem is particularly acute in California where in 1994 voters overwhelmingly approved Proposition 187 which denies public benefits to illegal aliens and their children. This has fostered the current negative tone of the national conversation about immigration and the crusade for a moratorium by conservative writers such as Peter Brimelow, an English immigrant, who, in *Alien Nation*, has argued for a temporary moratorium to allow local jurisdictions to absorb the large number of immigrants who have arrived since the middle of the 1960s. Brimelow bases his argument on the fact that the massive European migration to this country at the turn of the twentieth century was followed by a lull in immigration from the 1920s to the middle of the 1960s, allowing the various European ethnic groups to learn English and to become fully absorbed into the main stream of American culture. But Brimelow's real fear is that America might ultimately lose its identity as a predominantly white nation if present migration trends continue, because half of the net annual increase in the American population is made up of non-white immigrants (Brimelow 1995). Others fear that the sustained inflow of immigrants has led to an excessive preoccupation with multiculturalism, and therefore an emphasis on the *pluribus* in our national motto at the expense on the *unum*, and that if immigration is left unchecked, they argue, it may eventually lead to the balkanization of America.

Yet not all conservative writers call for a moratorium, even if they have concerns about the divisive implications of excessive multiculturalism. William J. Bennett, Secretary of Education in the Reagan Administration, for example, argues that "our problem does not have to do with legal immigration but with assimilation—and assimilation not just for people born in foreign lands but for people born in this nation" (Bennett 1994, p. C7). In commenting on the proposed reform of current immigration policy to restrict the inflow of immigrants, Bennett takes the traditional view of legal immigration: "While there are some minor reforms worth examining, my views on legal immigration are guided by an explicit underlying conviction: Legal immigrants are a net plus for America and hence current policy is essentially viable."

CONCLUDING COMMENTS

Every country has the right to control the number of people who enter its borders. But they also have obligations to the rest of the world. Some countries by virtue of their history and their commitment to freedom have more obligations than others. The United States has more obligation to the international movement of people than others because it can demonstrate more than most countries the benefits of immigration. And even though most Americans may view newly arrived immigrants as taking away low-wage jobs from native-born workers, the fact is that low-wage workers abroad are more responsible for those job losses because they attract American firms to produce offshore. Indeed, the globalization of the world economy has improved the mobility of capital far more than it has labor, and the new restrictive immigration bill now going through the Congress might very well encourage more businesses to take low-wage jobs abroad. This would be a blow to both low-wage immigrants and native-born workers.

Let me end by saying that immigrants come to America to improve the economic condition of their households and in the process they contribute to the cultural and economic wealth of the nation for generations to come. Many come with sophisticated skills. Others acquire these skills after they arrive. And still others who come with average skills toil anonymously in humble occupations. Peter Brimelow mocks what he calls the "anecdotal happy-talk good news coverage of immigration that we all know and love" such as some poor immigrant kid who couldn't speak English and rises to become valedictorian at Harvard (Brimelow 1995, p. 6). I wonder what Brimelow would say about some kid whose father came to America on a banana boat, who grew up in humble surroundings in the Bronx, who became the leader of the world's most powerful military, and who many believe would make an excellent candidate for the presidency of the United States?

REFERENCES

Bennett, William J. 1994. "Immigration: Making Americans," *The Washington Post*, December 4.

Brimelow, Peter. 1995. *Alien Nation*. New York: Random House.

Burtless, Gary, and Timothy Smeeding. 1995. *"America's Tide: Lifting the Yachts, Swamping the Rowboats,"* The Washington Post, June 25.

Gayle, Dennis, and Jonathan N. Goodrich (eds.). 1993. *Tourism Marketing and Management in the Caribbean*. New York: Routledge.

Huddle, Donald. 1995. *The Net National Costs of Immigration in 1994.* Washington, DC: Carrying Capacity Network.

Nossiter, Adam. 1995. "A Jamaican Way Station in the Bronx," *The New York Times*, October 25, Section B.

Palmer, Ransford W. 1995. *Pilgrims from the Sun: West Indian Migration to America*. New York: Twayne Publishers.

Sowell, Thomas. 1975. *Race and Economics*. New York: David McKay Co.

United States Bureau of the Census. 1990. *Profiles of Our Ancestry: Selected Characteristics by Ancestry Group*. CPH-L-149, Washington, DC: Government Printing Office.

United States Immigration and Naturalization Service. 1994. Washington, DC: Statistcal Division.

5

The Future of
U.S. Immigration Policy

Curtis A. Ward

What we can expect of U.S. Immigration law and policy in the future and how it will ultimately impact on the Western Hemisphere Region may be found in the pages of its historical development. There is evidence to support the conclusion that there is a strong correlation between the evolution of U.S. immigration policy and the economic and political dynamics of the period.

The U.S. Commission on Immigration Reform in its 1994 report to the Congress noted that immigration policies for the 1990s and beyond should anticipate the challenges of the twentieth century. The Commission suggested that such factors as the restructuring of the U.S. economy, the establishment of such new trade relationships as NAFTA, and changing geopolitical relations are important elements when considering the future of U.S. immigration policy. The Commission also noted that social concerns, demographic trends, and the impact of added population on the country's environment must be taken into consideration.

Because of the long history of the evolution of U.S. immigration law and policy, an understanding of that history will be extremely helpful not only by way of interpreting the present policy but also in predicting the future of U.S. immigration policy. Economic and political planners in the region, when assessing the impact of migration on the political and economic landscape, should also find it useful.

If we begin with the premise that immigration legislation in the U.S. Congress reflects the prevailing economic and political conditions of the day, we will not be surprised by the debate that is taking place today. Immigration legislation, and hence immigration policy, has shown two distinct patterns. Up until about 1875, immigration policy was one of tolerance and encouragement. Although there have been short periods of liberalization in U.S. immigration policy, there has been a general trend of ever-increasing restrictions post 1875.

During the first 100 years of the United States as a settler colony, the period was marked by unimpeded immigration. The gates were literally open, and all were welcome. The immigrants and their descendants were to a great extent major contributors to the growth of the young nation. One of the earliest attempts at restriction, the Alien Act of 1798, lapsed after two years because of its unpopularity. As late as 1864, Congress passed legislation to encourage immigration, and many of the individual states had programs to promote immigration. Needless to say, as it had been throughout the history of the United States, there were always small but vocal groups that actively opposed immigration even during that period.

With the enactment of the 1875 statute, U. S. immigration law and policy began creeping towards more and more restrictions. Convicts and prostitutes were the first to be barred, followed by a head tax of $.50, later increased to $8.00, as the list of excludable categories of immigrants grew. In 1882 the first race-based statute, the Chinese Exclusion Act, was enacted. This law remained in force until 1943.

As the U.S. economy grew and more frontiers were opened up, the Congress enacted contract labor laws in 1885 and 1887 that allowed for importation of cheap foreign labor into the United States. These contract labor laws were found to depress the U.S. labor market and were later repealed.

The year 1891 saw the enactment of a statute that in effect codified then existing immigration laws and policies, provided for medical inspection of immigrants, and further expanded the class of persons who were excludable from the United States. This was followed in 1903 by a law that, for the first time, added a political exclusion—that of anarchist. The legislative history suggests that this statute was a reflection of the political debate resulting from the assassination of President McKinley some 18 months earlier.

During the first ten years of the twentieth century, there was a massive increase in the number of immigrants primarily from southern and eastern Europe. Before this period most of the immigrants were from northern Europe. A period of economic instability also added to the great concern about this new group of immigrants. As a result of the intensity of the ensuing debate, a commission—The Dillingham Commission—was appointed in 1907 to review immigration law and policy, and after four years of study they issued an extensive report recommending restrictive measures, many of which were adopted in 1917 over the veto of President Wilson. The Act of February 5, 1917, resulted in a very comprehensive revision of the immigration laws. For the first time a literacy test was introduced, and it also created the Asiatic Barred Zone, aimed at shutting out Orientals.

A series of laws followed, such as the Anarchist Act of 1918 and the Quota Law of 1921. The latter, for the first time introduced numerical limitations in U.S. immigration policy. This quota law was passed in fear of the anticipated flood of post-World War I European refugees as well as concern over the postwar depression. The Act of May 26, 1924, which soon followed, permanently enshrined numerical limitations in U.S. immigration policy. Based on a national origin formula, which set a quota for each nationality on the number of persons of their national origin in the United States in 1920, the net result was considerably disadvantageous to southern and eastern European immigrants and provided significant advantages to northern Europeans. This law, however, also allowed entry of nationals of Western Hemisphere countries without restrictions but retained the bar to Orientals. Together the 1917 and 1924 acts provided the foundation of immigration law and policy, in terms of qualitative restrictions and numerical limitations.

Except for the Alien Registration Act of 1940—enacted during World War II, for obvious political and securityrelated reasons—which added subversive groups to the list of excludable immigrants, there were very limited changes in U.S. immigration law and policy for some time. The Internal Security Act of 1950, enacted during a period of strident political debate in the United States, expanded the exclusion and expulsion of subversives from the United States. Also, in the wake of World War II, the Displaced Persons Act of 1948 brought some 400,000 refugees from Europe.

The first major overhaul of U.S. immigration law and policy of the modern era was the McCarran-Walter Act, enacted over President Truman's veto on June 27, 1952. Although it has been amended on numerous occasions, it remained the basic statute governing immigration law and policy for many years.

One of its most important provisions related to the treatment it accorded to Western Hemisphere countries. It established annual quotas based on national origins for immigrants from all countries except those in the Western Hemisphere, who were exempted from the quotas. It also established racial quotas for Asians and a quota for skilledbased immigrants.

As had been the case leading up to that period, past presidents had turned to commissions to study and make recommendations for overhauling the immigration system. President Truman, stung by the Congress's override of his veto in enactment of the 1952 statute, appointed a special Commission on Immigration and Naturalization. The Commission, recognizing the race-based elements of U.S. immigration law and policy, issued a report sharply critical of the McCarran-Walter Act and strongly recommended numerous changes. Among these were to abolish the national origins system and to replace it with a unified quota system that allocates quotas without regard to national origin, race, creed, or color. Also, recognizing the political climate in which certain exclusions and deportations were taking place, the Commission recommended that the highest standards of fairness should apply in exclusion and deportation hearings along with a process for appellate review of such proceedings, and that arbitrary and unreasonable grounds, as were prevalent during the McCarthy era, be eliminated.

Needless to say, as a consequence of the prevailing political climate of the period, several attempts at major reform based on the Commission's report never made it through the Congress. President Kennedy's proposals in 1963, later adopted by President Johnson, followed closely the recommendations of the commission.

The result was the passage of the Act of October 3, 1965, which brought many important and comprehensive changes. Among these was the elimination of discrimination based on race or national origin. It, however, imposed restrictions on the entry of persons seeking to perform labor and restrictions on Western Hemisphere nationals. Immigration of nationals of the Western Hemisphere became subject to an annual quota of 120,000, and the rest of the world was set at an annual quota of 170,000. The law established a seven-category preference system, favoring close relatives of U.S. citizens and permanent residents as well as those with needed occupational skills.

In the case of skilled and unskilled labor, the Secretary of Labor had to first determine or certify that qualified U.S. workers were not available to perform the proposed employment and, further, that employment of such foreign nationals would not adversely affect wages and working conditions in the United States.

The period beginning with the U.S. entry into World War II had also provided for economic related changes in U.S. immigration law and policy. The U.S. economy was then in an economic upswing, and there was a shortage of labor, particularly in agriculture. It is instructive to note that in order to relieve the labor pressures of the period, the United States, in 1942, entered into bilateral agreements with Mexico, British Honduras (now Belize), Barbados, and Jamaica for entry of temporary foreign laborers to work in the United States under the so-called bracero program. This program was ended by the United States in 1964. The Chinese Exclusion Laws were also repealed in 1943.

In the aftermath of the Vietnam War, the Indochinese Refugees Resettlement Program was instituted. This was followed in 1976 by the imposition of per country limitations of 20,000 on Western Hemisphere countries. Also in 1976, on the basis of a legislative finding that there was no longer a shortage of doctors in the United States, a statute was enacted imposing severe restrictions on the entry of foreign doctors. In 1978 both the Western Hemisphere and the rest of the world were placed in an overall worldwide quota program. That same year Congress passed a law excluding and deporting Nazi persecutors.

The debate over immigration law and policy intensified in the latter part of the decade of the 1970s. In order to deal with the pressures for immigration reform, the Congress enacted legislation on October 5, 1978, that established the Select Commission on Immigration and Refugee Policy. There had not been a comprehensive review of immigration and refugee law and policy in over 30 years prior to that time.

The Select Commission was charged with undertaking a thorough examination of U.S. immigration policy, which was deemed imperative by the Congress in view of the significant changes in immigration pressures, public attitudes towards immigration, and the needs of society. The rising number of refugees throughout the world was also of major concern. The Mariel boat-lift, which resulted in tens of thousands of Cubans flooding the Florida coast, was to further exacerbate the problem.

During the period leading up to the establishment of the commission, demographic, economic, and political changes had taken place throughout the world, namely, post-World War II reconfiguration of Europe, the Korean War, the Vietnamese War, and the dismantling of colonialism.

The introduction to the Final Report of the Select Commission is, at the very least, instructive. It states in part:

It is a truism to say that the United States is a nation of immigrants, it is also a truism that it is one no longer, nor can it become a land of unlimited immigration. As important as immigration has been and remains to our country, it is no longer possible to say as George Washington did, that we welcome all of the oppressed of the world, or as did the poet, Emma Lazarus, that we should take all of the huddled masses yearning to be free.

The commission, recognizing that the United States exists in a shrinking, interdependent world; that world economic and political forces result in the migration of peoples; and that because many large-scale, international migrations are caused by war, poverty, and persecution within sending nations, it is in the national interest of the United States to work with other nations to prevent or ameliorate those conditions. The commission asked the question: Is immigration in the national interest? It answered with a strong but qualified "yes." Stating that there are many benefits that immigrants bring to U.S. society, noted, however, that there are limits on the ability of the United States to absorb large numbers of immigrants effectively. In the commission's words,

Immigrants, refugees and their children work hard and contribute to the economic well-being of our society; strengthen our social security system and manpower capability; strengthen our ties with other nations; increase our language and cultural resources and powerfully demonstrate to the world that the United States is an open and free society.

The commission made it clear that immigration policy must be guided by the basic national interests of the people of the United States. And that while providing opportunity for immigration, the United States must continue to have some limits.

The resulting commission's recommendations made in 1981, and the development of policy between that time and now, provide a useful guide as we contemplate the future of U.S. immigration policy. This is particularly so as the report placed emphasis on controlling immigration in the Western Hemisphere.

Of particular interest to the region is the recommendation with regard to matters of trade, aid, investment, and development. And as to another of its recommendations, that is, the legalization of a substantial portion of those who were already here in the U.S. for some time in an illegal status, the commission expressed the view that the process of legalization that would provide new and accurate information about the origins of migration, information which would allow the United States to target aid and investment programs to deal with migration pressures at the source.

It has been suggested that the Reagan administration reacted in part to the Commission's recommendations by conceiving of the Caribbean Basin Initiative (CBI) granting duty-free access to certain goods exported to the United States from designated Caribbean Basin countries. The CBI was supposed to create jobs in Caribbean Basin countries as investors were expected to take advantage of this new trading regime for goods produced there. The creation of jobs would invariably reduce migration pressures. However, as Dr. Ransford Palmer has accurately pointed out in *Pilgrims from the Sun* the CBI's explicit objective of expanding employment opportunities in CBI countries has had only limited success. And, the CBI's implicit objective, that of reducing migration to the United States, has been even less successful.

Three major pieces of immigration legislation were adopted from 1980 to 1990—the Refugee Act of 1980, the Immigration Reform and Control Act of 1986, and the Immigration Act of 1990. These laws invariably moved towards more restrictions on and greater controls of immigration, and stricter enforcement of immigration laws. The 1980 Refugee Act for the first time adopted the international definition of refugee, thereby rejecting the earlier U.S. definition of refugees as being individuals fleeing communist countries.

The U.S. Commission on Immigration Reform in its 1994 interim report to the Congress made recommendations aimed at curbing illegal immigration, including more vigorous enforcement of employer sanctions, a national verification system of employment authorization, speedier deportation of criminal aliens, a more efficient system of deportation of illegal aliens, and increased border enforcement capabilities.

The commission's report on legal immigration that is due in 1997 will no doubt follow its mandate, that is, make recommendations regarding the impact of immigration on family reunification; labor needs, employment, and other economic conditions; social relations; demographics; natural resources; and foreign policy and national security.

A brief examination of each of these elements of future immigration policy is germane to this discussion.

1. *Family reunification.* The commission will examine among other things the role of family reunification on the integration of new immigrants into U.S. society and to what extent the recent increases in naturalization will create greater demand for future admissions as the new citizens petition for their relatives.

2. *Impact on labor needs, employment and other economic conditions in the United States.* The commission will examine both the short and long-term effects of immigration on the labor market. Specifically, the commission will examine the characteristics of immigrants as they relate to U.S. labor market considerations—education, skill level, occupation, employment experience, etc., having entered their labor force participation rate, employment, earnings, and job mobility experience by

different categories of immigrants; the impact of immigrants on the labor force participation rate, employment and earnings of domestic workers (by race, ethnicity, and citizenship); the impact of immigrants in different categories on the working conditions and benefits of domestic workers; the type and impact of entrepreneurial activities in which immigrants engage; and the effects of immigrants on specific industries.

3. *Social and community relations.* The commission will examine the effects of the immigrant population on social and community relations; the civic integration of immigrants, including participation in local, state, and national political constituencies, and other manifestations of civic involvement. In other words the level of involvement of immigrants in the U.S. political process will be examined.

4. *Demographics.* The commission will examine the effects of immigration on overall demographic trends and the ethnic, racial, and age composition of the U.S. population; and they will examine data to predict future demographics. Such data will include a study of the fertility rate of immigrants in their country of origins. This will help policymakers determine to what extent immigrants will contribute to the racial and ethnic composition of the United States in the years ahead, which is obviously of major concern to policy makers.

5. *Environment.* The commission will seek to determine whether environmental problems in the sending countries are related to immigration. It will also examine the environmental impact of immigrants on U.S. communities.

6. *Foreign policy and national security.* The commission will examine a host of foreign policy and national security issues related to immigration. These will include:

   a. migration trends from countries in which the United States has a foreign policy interest.

   b. the relationships in both directions between U.S. immigration policy and U.S. foreign economic policies, that is, on trade, aid, and investment, and in particular impacts upon trade relationships.

   c. the impact of migration upon U.S. foreign policy, including the role played by immigrants and refugees in influencing U.S. policy with regard to the countries of their births or ethnicity.

   d. the impact of changes in U.S. immigration policy on countries of origin or third countries, with resulting implications for U.S. relationships with those countries.

e. the impact of U.S. foreign policy on international migration and refugee flows.

f. the effects of U.S. refugee policies on U.S. foreign policy objectives.

g. the appropriateness of various foreign policy initiatives to prevent or deter mass migration.

h. transnational issues of international migration and refugee movements, including regional safe haven arrangements.

i. the security aspects of immigration.

The commission will also look at the impact of highly skilled labor migration to the United States on the countries of origin as it relates to foreign policy.

What are some of the conclusions to be derived from all of this with regard to the future of U.S. immigration policy? The debates taking place will undoubtedly influence the findings, conclusions, and recommendations of the commission. We can expect the trend towards increased border enforcement and stricter enforcement of employment laws to continue with greater urgency. On the domestic fronts we can expect politicians, depending on which end of the political spectrum they appear, to base their positions on whether current legal immigration poses a real threat to the majority population both in terms of its composition with regard to ethnicity and race and also on whether civic participation by immigrants, as they become citizens, could invariably affect the political landscape one way or another.

There has never been an undertaking of this magnitude by any previous commission as to the relationship between immigration and the foreign and national security policies of the United States. Immigration policy in the past has been based mostly on reaction to the prevailing conditions of the period. This ongoing comprehensive study is also a reaction to certain discernible trends. However, policymakers hope that the findings and recommendations of the ommission will provide the basis for proactive measures. The findings will undoubtedly be taken into consideration in formulation of future hemispheric policy. In particular it will be used in the formulation of negotiating positions as the region moves towards a hemispheric free-trade area.

We have seen that even predating the commission's findings and recommendations, environmental and labor conditions were made a part of NAFTA. As we move forward in the process towards free trade, the United States will no doubt seek to have Caribbean Basin countries and other countries in the region pursue economic policies aimed at reducing migration pressures. Certainly, future U.S. trade, aid, and investment concessions may be predicated on a country's or the region's response to reducing migration pressures on the United States. On the U.S. side, we can expect reductions in legal immigration to continue into the twenty-first century.

6

Exporting Culture: Caribbean Americans in New York City

Joyce Toney

INTRODUCTION

There is general agreement among economists and other social scientists that the Caribbean nations are poor in natural resources. Except for bauxite in Jamaica and Guyana, petroleum in Trinidad, and the unpredictable tourist industry, these countries have little that is coveted by the wider world.[1] Yet in spite of that material poverty, people on all continents know and recognize the increasing influence of Caribbean culture on their own music and life-styles.[2]

The West Indian Commission drew reference to the importance of culture as a means of development when it recommended that "the potential for employment-creation via the promotion of cultural industries be addressed by both the private sector and the Governments of CARICOM Member Countries as part of their strategies for attracting investment capital inflows; (and) that there also be an analysis of the global environment for trade in cultural industry services."[3]

There is strong evidence that Caribbean leaders and governments share this view about the export of culture. For example, they view the individual carnivals held in the islands as a major boost to their economies. As a result, each island celebrates Carnival at a different time of the year instead of on the traditional day before Ash Wednesday.

In 1995 the Minister of culture in St. Vincent and the Grenadines visited Toronto and New York City to encourage Vincentian nationals and others to visit for Carnival.[4] Jamaica, an island that has not had the same tradition of Carnival, recognized the benefits to be gained and began a successful festival in 1991 as an attempt to add to its tourist industry.

Within the last 20 years, however, another phenomenon has been taking place. There has been an upsurge of Caribbean-style Carnival in the major cities of the metropolitan countries. In their effort to re-create a bit of the home society, West Indians abroad have transplanted Carnival culture and have turned it into an essential aspect of life overseas.

West Indian-style carnivals are celebrated in North America, England, and the continent of Europe. In the United States alone, Carnivals are held in New York, Boston, Miami, Washington, Detroit, and Philadelphia.[5] This paper focuses on the Carnival held on Labor Day in Brooklyn, New York. The aim is to demonstrate the ways in which Carnival helped to attract attention to West Indian culture, to the migrant community, and to the societies from which the migrants came.

West Indians in New York and at home benefit from the financial and political consequences of what is perceived to be a highly successful attempt to market culture and build an integrated community. Their original goal was simply a continuation of their culture in their adopted homelands,[6] but in fact there have been other results. Throughout the years there has been greater contact between the migrants and their home societies through the music and culture that transcend national borders. Consequently there has been an increasing visibility of West Indian culture in New York and an expanded market for the cultural commodities originating in the Caribbean.

The benefits to the Caribbean can be observed in at least two different arenas:[7] (1) There are the financial and marketing opportunities accruing to Caribbean artists and entrepreneurs at home and abroad; and (2) there is the augmented political clout brought to the Caribbean community. The latter assumption is also based on the premise that the activities, successes, and failures of an immigrant community directly affect the home societies. This phenomenon has been present in American society from its inception. American ethnic groups including the Germans, Italians, Poles, and Jews have played major roles in directing the relationships between their home societies and the United States.[8] Currently we are witnessing the influence of Irish Americans in the peace process between Northern Ireland and Britain.

ORIGIN OF WEST INDIAN CARNIVAL IN NEW YORK

The Caribbean-style Carnival first appeared in the New York community with the arrival of the calypsonian. By 1915 the song "Sly Mongoose" was on American phonograph records. In the early decades of the twentieth century an estimated 80,000 to 90,000 West Indians arrived in the United States.[9] By the 1930s Trinidad calypso was gaining popularity with American audiences. Artists included Sam Manning, Lionel Belasco, Gerald Clark, and the very popular Houdini.

After 1965, large numbers of new immigrants who benefited from the 1965 United States Immigration Act moved to Brooklyn. The number of immigrants from the Caribbean increased dramatically. Between 1967 and 1976, 229,000 West Indians immigrated into the United States.[10] Of the 953,000 immigrants who entered New York City between 1980 and 1990, over one-third were West Indian. During the same time 205,000 of the overall immigrant population who came to Brooklyn were West Indian.[11]

It was during this period of expanding migration that the Carnival was moved from Harlem to Brooklyn under the leadership of Rufus Goring. Goring and his group struggled continuously to gain the legitimacy that was necessary to conduct a successful Carnival. On one occasion he was arrested for holding the Carnival without a permit. Eventually, however, the organizers finally acquired annual permits to hold the Carnival on Eastern Parkway. Carlos Lezama, who has been at the head of the West Indian American Day Carnival Association (WIADCA) since then, played a major role in acquiring the permit. Today, the West Indian day carnival attracts over 1 million spectators, and is reputed to be the largest parade in the United States.

THE MARKETING OF SOCA AND CALYPSO

West Indians, at home and abroad, recognize the financial benefits to be gained from Labor Day Carnival and its by-products. The
success of Labor Day Carnival has spawned other outlets for
Caribbean culture. Eastern Parkway on Labor Day is the venue of
a number of budding entrepreneurs. Vendors, Caribbean and non-
Caribbean, take advantage of the opportunities to peddle their
wares. This is a time, too, when other New Yorkers become introduced to the varieties of Caribbean food, arts, and crafts.[12] Similarly, more-established Caribbean and American businesses
sponsor Carnival bands as a form of advertisement.

Labor Day Carnival contributed to the resuscitation of West
Indian, particularly Eastern Caribbean, Soca and calypso culture in
New York. Caribbean culture continues to be popular throughout
the year. Soca music is played in practically all of the clubs in New
York. West Indian young people are not embarrassed to identify
with the music of their parents. The visibility and pride of the
revelers on Labor Day Carnival perpetuate the West Indian tradition in which Carnival is a link between generations.

Labor Day Carnival led to other media for disseminating Caribbean culture. *Everybody's*, a Caribbean American magazine
launched by Grenadian Herman Hall, has been published continuously for an unprecedented 19 years. Hall admits that the magazine
was founded in the annual Labor Day Brooklyn Carnival. He was
one of the members of the executive board of the WIADCA, the
group that organized the Carnival.

West Indian performers living at home have not been reluctant
to take advantage of the growing opportunities outside the region.
They recognize that the high quality of Caribbean music and
culture has not been duplicated outside of the islands. The best is
still at home. Since the 1980s, visiting bands from the Caribbean
including Catelli All Stars Steel Band from Trinidad and Tobago
and Byron Lee and the Dragonaires have been part of the show on
the road. Calypsonians recognize the importance of the show and
cater to the audiences, as evidenced by Sparrow's "Mas in Brooklyn," and Rootsman's "Eastern Parkway Jam Back."

Musical bands come from all of the islands, sponsored by the
nationals of different Caribbean countries. Some of the bands con-

tinue to perform at dances and other performances in New York and then move on to Caribana in Toronto in August. Similarly, costume designers come to New York to ply their trade, and they improve the quality of New York-based Carnival bands. Master costume designer Stephen Lee Hueng was invited to New York by the popular children's steel band "Sesame Flyers."[13]

POLITICS AND THE WEST INDIAN CARNIVAL

By the end of the 1960s large numbers of West Indian homeowners and tenants settled in the deteriorating buildings of Crown Heights.[14] This was accompanied by a mass exodus of whites from the community. Because the Lubavitcher Hasidim Jewish community, still residing in Crown Heights, objected to what they perceived to be the intrusion of the Carnival on Labor Day, Lezama and his people had to work hard to convince the authorities otherwise. Their work was made doubly difficult because politicians had praised the decision made by the Lubavitchers to stay in the area, and were committed to helping them remain.[15]

The fact that these issues were played out and resolved in public helped to push the West Indian community onto the forefront of the New York political scene. In 1971 *The New York Times* covered Labor Day Carnival, and since that time businesses and civic organizations have played a major role in the parade.[16] In 1995, for the first time, the festival was carried live on local New York television.

The rising attention given to Carnival was partly a result of the increased political clout of the Caribbean community in New York. Caribbean migrants were perceived as being aggressive, upwardly mobile people who were making a mark on the Brooklyn community.[17] Shirley Chisholm's candidacy for the United States presidency in 1968 helped to give publicity to the community. Although Chisholm was identified as an African-American candidate, the media was not unmindful of her Caribbean origins and the growing strength of the people behind it.[18]

Before the new immigration of the late 1960s Caribbean politicians did not emphasize their immigrant status, rather they identified with the issues facing the larger Black community.[19] The new immigration ushered in a more selfconscious, openly proud immigrant politician, willing to cater to the growing Caribbean vote.

African-American politicians, who had always shared a political stage with West Indian politicians,[20] were among the first group to recognize the growing importance of the new migrant Caribbean community. African-American politicians had been accused by Caribbean leaders of ignoring immigration issues and other causes peculiar to immigrants. These leaders recognized the rapidly increasing numbers of Caribbean people living among them and made an effort to understand their peculiar concerns.

One of the first and most prominent African-American politicians to take advantage of the political mileage emanating from Carnival was Rev. Jesse Jackson. He and other politicians used the opportunity to encourage West Indians and African-Americans to register to vote. In 1984 he used the wrong approach by failing to give the expected amount of attention to the organizers of Carnival. By 1988, however, Jackson had learned his lessons, and he received a rousing welcome from the crowd. In 1993 he marched in a delegation that included Miss Trinidad and Tobago, Miss Guiness Gold, and Carlos Lezama.[21]

Similarly, David Dinkins, the first elected black Mayor of New York, seized the opportunity to embrace Black New York on Labor Day. In 1993, in his bid for reelection, Mayor Dinkins "walked the 20 block length of the parade where colorful island creations preceded him. Surrounded by 'Dinkins for Mayor Signs,' the celebrants shouted their choice for 'four more years.' "[22]

Black politicians, considered more radical, have also used the parade as a forum. Leaders such as Al Sharpton, Rev. Herbert Daughtry, and Sonny Carson have all appeared and made formal statements at the parade. It was also during this period that WLIB, the African-American owned radio station, began to cover Carnival live, interviewing revelers on the street.

White politicians also recognize the importance of the Labor Day Carnival. They consider the festival to be a major city event, and every year the official launching of Carnival takes place at Gracie mansion, the official residence of the Mayor of New York City.[23] Furthermore, much of the official early fundraising takes place in public places such as the Brooklyn Museum under the auspices of the Brooklyn Borough President, Howard Golden.

The politician who has manipulated West Indian culture to the hilt is Martin Markowitz, State Senator from Brooklyn. Markowitz, a Jew, heads the predominantly Black district, which encompasses the predominantly white Midwood and the predominantly Black Crown Heights. Markowitz has been able to maintain a comfortable seat in the legislature in spite of some grumbling from some Caribbean leaders and a few half-hearted attempts to unseat him as the Democratic Party candidate.[24]

One of his strengths is the way in which he caters to the Caribbean community by embracing its culture, at least in public. The senator sponsors two sets of concerts every summer, one in Crown Heights featuring black artists and the other in Midwood featuring white artists. After several weeks of jazz, rhythm and blues, and pop music, the grand finale of the black concerts is the appearance of Mighty Sparrow and other West Indian artists. Markowitz always acts as the Master of Ceremonies, introducing all of the performers, and when Sparrow takes the stage, he performs with him for a few minutes. This concert takes place immediately before Labor Day and sets the tone for the Carnival functions, at which Senator Markowitz also appears. It is difficult to determine the extent to which his clowning and camaraderie impress the audience, but Markowitz has managed to maintain political power in the community.

During the 1970s and 1980s the presence of the competing Labor Day parade sponsored by New York labor unions on fifth Avenue in New York City helped to cloud the visibility of Carnival on Eastern Parkway. In 1994, for the first time, there was no labor union parade in Manhattan. As a result all politicians, Republicans and Democrats, attended only the West Indian Day parade in Brooklyn. This event, more than any other, can be seen as the virtual coming of age of Labor Day Carnival. In a front page story in the *New York Times* there was a picture of Black activist Lenora Fulani and former Governor Mario Cuomo, both contenders for the New York State governorship, marching in the parade. At one point, the former governor, who is known for his use of humor, was asked the day before if he planned to attend the parade. He said "Of course, I'm from Jamaica. That's Jamaica, Queens."[25]

The governor's remarks drew attention to the growing importance of the Caribbean community. State Senator Marty Markowitz was quoted as saying, "There was a time when there was Italy,

Ireland, and Israel from New York City. Now you have to add on the Caribbean as a major power center. There's a growing recognition that the West Indian community has become one of the most important political forces in the country."[26]

CONCLUSION

Although economic success has largely eluded the new Caribbean nations, the countries have been highly successful at marketing their music and other cultural forms abroad. Labor Day Carnival in Brooklyn is one example that demonstrates the methods by which West Indians at home and abroad have drawn attention to one product that they have to offer and, consequently, to themselves. Caribbean people use Carnival as a means of exposing others to their rich culture. Although the culture brokers recognize that there is still much work to be done,[27] West Indians in New York and at home benefit politically, economically, and socially from the disseminating of their culture abroad.

NOTES

1. See for example Clive Y. Thomas, *The Poor and the Powerless: Economic Policy and Change in the Caribbean* (New York: Monthly Review Press, 1988); Carmen Diana Deere et al., in *The Shadows of the Sun: Caribbean Development Alternatives and U. S. Policy.* (Boulder: Westview Press, 1990); Stanley Lalta and Marie Freckleton, *Caribbean Economic Development: The First Generation* (Kingston: Ian Randle Publishers, 1993); Elsie Le Franc ed. *Consequences of Structural Adjustment: A Review of the Jamaican Experience* (Barbados: Canoe Press, 1994).

2. Kathy McAfee, *Storm Signals: Structural Adjustment and Development Alternatives in the Caribbean* (Boston: South End Press, 1991), 201–5.

3. Report of The West Indian Commission, *Time For Action* (Blackrock, Barbados, 1992), 305.

4. Council of St. Vincent and the Grenadines, USA, "Open Discussion," Culture Minister John Home, Friends of Crown Heights Day Care Center, Brooklyn, March 24, 1995.

5. Frank E. Manning, "Overseas Caribbean Carnivals: The Art and Politics of a Transnational Celebration," in Thomas M. Fiehrer and Michael W. Loderick (eds.), *Plantation Society in the Americas*, 1990, p. 47.

6. Robert Tomasson, "A Festival in Brooklyn Salutes West Indians With Calypso Beat," *The New York Times,* September 6, 1971, 23. Joseph Mitchell, "Houdini's Picnic." *The New Yorker,* May 6, 1939, reprinted in *Everybody's* (February 1982), 35–36

7. There is also evidence of increased unity and cohesion between different Caribbean nations in New York resulting from the parade, but this paper will not focus on that subject.

8. John Bodnar, *The Transplanted: A History of Immigrants in Urban America* (Bloomington: Indiana University Press, 1985).

9. Reeda Ueda, "West Indians," in Stephan Thernstrom et al. (eds.), *Harvard Encyclopedia of American Ethnic Groups* (Cambridge: Harvard University Press, 1980), 1022.

10. Isaac Dookhan, *The United States in the Caribbean* (London: Collins Caribbean, 1985), 99.

11. United States Census, 1990.

12. Mathew Purdy, *The New York Times,* September 6, 1994, B3, 1.

13. "New York Carnival 93," *Everybody's,* September 1993, 9.

14. Ibid.

15. Ibid., 7.

16. Robert E. Tomasson, "A Festival in Brooklyn Salutes West Indians With Carnival Beat," *The New York Times,* September 6, 1971, 23.

17. Thomas Sowell, *Essays and Data on American Ethnic Groups* (Washington, DC: The Urban Institute, 1978); Nathan Glazer and Daniel P. Moynihan, *Beyond the Melting Pot: The Negroes, Puerto Ricans, Jews and the Irish of New York City,* 2nd edition (Cambridge: M.I.T. Press, 1974).

18. Manning, 55; Shirley Chisholm, *Unbought and Unbossed* (Boston: Houghton Mifflin Company, 1970).

19. Ibid; Shirley Chisholm, *The Good Fight* (New York, Harper & Row, 1973), 15.

20. Calvin Holder, "The Rise and Fall of West Indian Politicians in New York City, 1900–1987," in George A. Irish and E. W. Riviere, (eds.), *Political Behavior and Social Interaction: Caribbean and African American Residents in New York* (Caribbean Research Center, Medgar Evers College, CUNY, 1980), 5–25.

21. Philip Kasinitz, *Caribbean New York: Black Immigrants and the Politics of Race* (Ithaca: Cornell University Press, 1992).

22. Manning, 55.

23. J. Zambga Browne and Vinette K. Pryce, "Dinkins hears 'Four More Years,' " *New York Amsterdam News,* September 11, 1993, 36.

24. Kasinitz, 238–46.

25. Matthew Purdy, "Parade Shows Off West Indian Political Clout," *The New York Times,* September 6, 1994, B3, 1.

26. Ibid, 1, 6.

27. Ralston Charles, Speech delivered at *Everybody's* Magazine, 1995 Calypso Awards, May 12, 1995.

7

From CBI to ACS:
Some Cultural Dimensions

Errol Miller

INTRODUCTION

Some time after the Caribbean Basin Initiative (CBI) was inaugurated by the United States, the Canadians followed with the Caribbean Canada agreement, CARIBCAN. One, obviously biased, commentator opined that the region had been downgraded from a basin to a can. The Association of Caribbean States, ACS, seems to have dispensed with the metallic metaphor linked to initiative and agreement, opting instead for the more organic imagery of an association. Interestingly, this conception is emerging from within the Caribbean, but the extent to which this will make any difference is still to be determined.

SOME BROAD CONSIDERATIONS

The fact that the Caribbean is subdivided culturally into Dutch-, English-, French-, and Spanish-speaking subgroups has nothing to do with the Caribbean itself. These cultural subdivisions are the legacy, if not the scars, of past European imperial occupation as they contested geopolitical advantage in bygone eras. It is testimony also of the strategic importance of the region in geopolitics of the past. In the contemporary context of globalization and the concomitant incipient emergence of mega-trading blocks, the Caribbean at the end of the twentieth century is faced with the challenge of reconfiguring itself to bring about greater unity and integration notwithstanding the diversity of its past.

DEFINING THE CARIBBEAN

Given its past history, the term Caribbean has always been variously defined. In many instances the Spanish-speaking countries of the region are grouped as Latin America. In these circumstances the Caribbean is defined as the Dutch-speaking territories of Aruba, the Netherlands Antilles, and Suriname; the French-speaking territories of Haiti, Guadeloupe, and Martinique; and the seventeen English-speaking countries that identify themselves as the Commonwealth Caribbean. There are numerous occasions when the English-speaking group appropriates the name for itself. Accordingly, the definition of the subregion can shift with the situation. In essence, therefore, the Caribbean is variously defined with respect to politics, geography, and culture. This explains why the South American countries of Guyana and Suriname, and Belize in Central America, are often classified with the Caribbean, while Cuba and the Dominican Republic are designated Latin America in similar circumstances. The cultural divisions, labeled by language, of the geographical Caribbean, Central America, and South America are real barriers to relationship in a common neighborhood.

In addition to the past cultural relationships marked by language, there are current political factors that also determine any working definition of the Caribbean. Aruba and the Netherlands Antilles are part of the Kingdom of the Netherlands. Martinique and Guadeloupe are departments of France. Puerto Rico is a commonwealth within the United States. Anguilla, Bermuda, British Virgin Islands, Cayman Islands, Montserrat, Turks and Caicos Islands are dependencies of Britain. Though being located in the Caribbean Sea geographically, their primary political relationships are with major industrial powers not considered part of the region.

The point is that within each cultural group there are territories that retain some form of political relationship with imperial powers of the past and present, and others are politically independent. The intersection of culture and politics within the region produces its own desiderata of relationships that have not only distorted and complicated past efforts of regional integration but promise to impose their own intriguing dimensions on the Association of Caribbean States. Interestingly, the Convention of the ASC offers Associate membership to the non-independent states, provided they apply for the same.

The contemporary importance of the non-independent states of the region can be illustrated by the fact that in the mid-1980s a standing joke in the Netherlands Antilles was a letter written by the Dutch government to the Antillian authorities stating that if they did not come for talks leading to political independence by a certain date, the instruments of political sovereignty would be sent to them by mail. By the end of the decade, neither had the Antillian representatives gone for independence, nor had the instruments been sent by mail as promised. One factor in the turnaround appeared to have been the recognition of the strategic importance of these micro states of the Caribbean. While still being part of Europe politically, they are geographically and culturally located in the midst of the emerging regional trading block of the Americas. By maintaining the European connections, these non-independent states, depending on one's perspective, are either toeholds in enemy territory or bridges between the trade blocks.

The Convention establishing the ACS has adopted its own working definition of the region within the context of its political realities. Roughly speaking, the Caribbean is defined as all the independent Caribbean countries washed by the Caribbean Sea except the United States. Hence it includes all the independent island countries, plus all the Central American countries, together with Mexico from the north and Columbia, Guyana, Suriname and Venezuela from the south. Associate membership is offered to the six British dependencies; Aruba and the Netherlands Antilles of the Kingdom of the Netherlands; the French departments of Guadeloupe, Martinique, and Guyane; and Puerto Rico. It will be Britain, the Netherlands, France, and the United States that will sign on behalf of these political entities. The point worth noting is that the ACS has employed the most inclusive definition of the Caribbean that has yet been adopted in any formal organization. However, remnants of past imperial politics persist to differentiate Caribbean states into two categories, full and associate members. It also opens the door for European and American involvement directly in councils of the Association with no reciprocity accorded to the region in comparable councils in Europe and the United States.

Cuba's membership of the ACS has prompted the United States to refrain from giving approval for the U.S. Virgin Islands and Puerto Rico to apply for Associate membership. In any case Puerto Rico is actively pursuing statehood and may not consider membership in the ACS as either prudent or necessary at the time. In other words, current global and regional politics have already constrained the definition of the Caribbean the ACS has sought to employ.

THE BROAD PARAMETERS OF CARIBBEAN CULTURE

The situation of the non-independent states of the Caribbean highlights one of the defining features of the Americas: its Eurocentric cultural orientation at a distance. From the time Columbus, and other Iberian explorers, connected the Americas with Western Europe, this hemisphere has been a part of the West culturally, though at a geographical distance. The evolution of this relationship has reached the point where the United States is now the leader of the Western World. In other words, the geopolitical center of gravity of the West is no longer located geographically in Europe but has been relocated in North America. Though this is a dramatic illustration of the relationship of the Americas with Western Europe and Western civilization, it must be recognized that in less dramatic but no less real terms the rest of the Americas continues to manifest this dualistic but intriguing relationship with Western Europe and Western culture.

The nature of Caribbean society and culture has been the subject of great debate among its scholars. Nettleford (1978) maintained that there are at least three cultural spheres, evident in different degrees, which in their interaction define the Americas:

- Plantation America, brutalized and ravaged and for that reason endemically rebellious, perennially resilient, and consistently creative

- Mestizo-America, valiantly resistant to the onslaught of European "discovery" and correspondingly majestic in its ancestral certitude
- Euro-America, still the active and often assertive purveyor of the ideas and technology of the conqueror forebearers and therefore reflective of that ambiance with which any thrust towards regional cooperation must contend

M. G. Smith (1965), when applying the theory of cultural pluralism to the Caribbean, maintained that the different cultural spheres and segments, to which Nettleford alluded, are marked by race and are sufficiently discrete and isolated by the institutional structures that perpetuate them as to require force as the means of ensuring social order. In other words, M. G. Smith insisted that the social and cultural cleavages in Caribbean societies were such that there was no normative consensus, and without the exercise of force by the dominant segments, the societies would descend into chaos. Although the reality of M. G. Smith's assertion that the stratification of Caribbean society was based primarily on cultural segments marked by race cannot be denied, the social cataclysm that he predicted has not yet materialized.

R. T. Smith (1967) posited a different interpretation, in which he maintained that Caribbean societies were evolving through various cultural forms—mainly, the plantation society of slavery, the Creole society of colonialism, and finally into the modern society of the postwar period. According to R. T. Smith modern society in the Caribbean was evolving into one based upon normative consensus and social integration underpinned by common institutions, values and interests, and social mobility based upon merit. Although R. T. Smith's analysis of Caribbean society and culture may not have been as penetrative as that of M. G. Smith, its more-optimistic predictions concerning the latter half of the twentieth century have largely been sustained. In the latter half of the twentieth century a significant measure of social and cultural integration has occurred based upon common educational and political institutions promoting the acceptance of common values and shared outlooks on the part of larger numbers of Caribbean people than ever before. At the same time, at the end of the century the process is far from complete, and elements of the plural past are still evident.

The contemporary global trend of regional integration, as epito-
mized and led by the European Union, emphasizes an inward- not
an outward-looking perspective. In addition it encompasses much
more than economic cooperation and trade. Central to the concept
of the European Union is the notion of the unification of Europe
through economic, political, social, and cultural institutions. Two
world wars and the Cold War have combined to foster the idea of
European unity as a defense against such recurrence in the future.

Even though NAFTA signals a similar move in economic terms,
NAFTA does not embody the similar political or cultural assumptions and goals. There is no corresponding notion of the unification
of the Americas politically, socially, and culturally. NAFTA is about
economics and trade without any presumptions of uniting the
peoples of the hemisphere. It is about material well-being without
any declared intentions concerning the psyche or the soul of the
hemisphere.

The Americas has yet to overcome the divisiveness of its past
and to look within itself collectively with a view to affirming and
enhancing its shared cultural dimensions. There is a very real sense
in which a culture of the Americas, an American culture, is very
much a work in the very early stages of the definition of its
contours. By a culture of the Americas or American culture, I mean
that which is founded upon and rooted in the mix of multicultural
inputs of all the peoples of the Americas and fashioned by the
realities of this hemisphere.

The Americas is unique in that there is no *Homo sapiens ameri-
canensis,* that is, no aboriginal peoples who can trace ancestry to
some primitive primate. All the peoples of this hemisphere are Old
World peoples relocated by choice or coercion, beginning with
Asians who emigrated across the northern land bridges in the
ancient past. They were indeed the first Americans—Old World
peoples remaking themselves in the New World.

English-speaking North America has practiced the Anglo-ver-
sion of Western culture with virtually no accommodation to culture
of the earliest Americans whom Columbus, in a quandary concerning his location, mistakenly called Indians. The dominance of
Anglo-European culture has existed within the context of European numerical dominance within the United States and Canada.
Hence all its interactions have been with the cultures of minority

groups, particularly the African-American minority. Even then the overriding principle of the melting pot has been to melt all into the Anglo-European mold. Though multiculturalism has emerged with strong supporters in the latter part of the twentieth century, the melting pot metaphor and its assumptions of a single culture still evoke strong passions.

In the rest of continental America, from Mexico to Chile, the Iberian version of Western European culture has been dominant. With the exception of Argentina and, and to a lesser extent, Chile, the country with major characteristics of cultural interaction, in this part of the Americas, with Western civilization and the first Americans. Accordingly, mestizo culture is a major component of what is generally referred to as Latin American. In other words, a defining difference between the North and South in the Americas is the intersection and interaction of the imposed culture of Western Europe and the culture of the first Americans.

In the cultural panorama of the Americas, the Caribbean presents some unique differences. First, though it shares with the rest of the Americas the historical dominance of Western European culture, the region harbors a wider mix of variants in terms of the particular variant that dominates, whether that be Anglo, French, Dutch, or Spanish. Second, with the exception of a few islands, the culture of the first Americans is almost nonexistent by virtue of their early extinction in this region. Third, the intersection and interactions of the various versions of European culture have been with the cultures of Africa and Asia, particularly India. Fourth, though Western European culture has been dominant, the European elements of Caribbean societies have been minorities within African and Asian majorities. Indeed, the Caribbean is the only region outside of Africa where people of African ancestry constitute the majority. These four features of the Caribbean, combined with its peculiar island geography, create a cultural kaleidoscope that is unique not only in the Americas but in the world.

Caribbean uniqueness and diversity present their own peculiar challenges to unity, integration, and cooperation. To begin with, the four different European points of reference, rooted in the colonial history, have fostered a tendency to look outside of the region for paradigms of action. Also each promoted its own cultural center, whether Madrid, Paris, Amsterdam, or London, and was chauvinistic in adhering to claims of its own superiority. Palacio (1990), in his study of social mobility in Belize, found that persons of Spanish ancestry were constrained to give up their "Spanishness" in order to ascend the socioeconomic ladder in the British colony.

The European cultural and colonial masters also encouraged bilateral relationships between themselves and their colonies but discouraged interaction between those colonies and their geographical neighbors of other cultural groups. That is, as competing versions of a common Western civilization, they have discouraged contact and intercourse between their cultural competitors within the region. In addition, the African and Indian majorities have continually had to withstand assertions branding their ancestral culture as inferior, resist attempts to suppress their heritage, and contend with channels of mobility that offer economic advancement in exchange for mastery of the dominant culture and abandonment of ancestral languages. Also the dominant minorities have always maintained their position by alliances with and assistance from sources external to the region. The tendencies are still evident in the era of political independence. It is a legacy that the ACS has inherited and ignores only to its peril.

THE ASSOCIATION OF CARIBBEAN STATES AND CULTURE

The Association of Caribbean States adds further cultural diversity to the Caribbean by its wider definition, which includes Venezuela, Columbia, Mexico, and the countries of Central America, with their dominant mestizo culture. Even though Belize has always been included in the Caribbean fraternity, the intercourse with Central America, with the exception of Panama, has been spasmodic and sometimes minimal. The ACS, for the first time, attempts to bring Mestizo America into formal relationship with Plantation America in this geographical intersection between the North and South of the hemisphere.

It is important to note that the motivation is largely that of economic necessity within the context of global trends. Of the five committees to be established, three focus on matters germane to economics; one is mandated to address administration issues; and the fifth combines science, technology, education, health, and culture. It is not unreasonable to say that while the Convention reveals nodding recognition of these latter areas, it has unequivocally established its priority as economics and trade.

The ACS is more a response to global economic imperatives than an intuitive invention of the Caribbean in search of greater inclusion of its Latin neighbors. Ironically it is European unity via the North American NAFTA response that has stimulated Caribbean reaction in the form of the ACS. Accordingly, the ACS is largely a creation of the governments with little knowledge and even less understanding of its purpose by ordinary citizens.

Interestingly, the ACS has come in the wake of three regional organizations with represented mechanisms of linking the region to major trading partners. First was the Caribbean Basin Initiative, CBI, establishing preferential access to the American market. Second was the CARIBCAN arrangement, with established parallel preferences for the region in the Canadian market. Third was the Lomé Convention, and within it CARIFORUM, which links the Caribbean to the European Union. The main point to note is that each of these is basically a trading protocol that assumes substantial and independent cultural connections and understanding as its context. These assumptions of substantial independent cultural connections are well founded, given the past history of the region in relation to Europe and the long-standing connections with North America.

The ACS is not a trading protocol. Neither does it link subregions with strong cultural connections among themselves. Although they share a common history of slavery and colonialism, differences in colonial masters have conspired to keep these geographical neighbors as virtual economic strangers and distant cultural cousins. This is not to say that there are no people connections across the cultural subgroups within the Caribbean and Central America.

Beginning with the building of railroads in Central America in the latter half of the nineteenth century, Caribbean people have emigrated within the region. English-speaking cultural enclaves within Honduras, Nicaragua, Costa Rica, Cuba, and Panama testify to these movements. Similarly the fact that English is the lingua franca in St. Martin, Saba, and St. Eustatius in the Netherlands Antilles not only reflects their proximity to English-speaking islands but also to the movement of people between them. Likewise, movements of Spanish- and French-speaking peoples punctuate the history of many English-speaking islands.

From George Lisle and Moses Baker who started the Baptist work in Jamaica to Father Richard Albert working in the inner city of Kingston, from Marcus Garvey to Louis Farrakan who have led mass movements in America, and from Claude McKay to Derek Walcott whose literary works have crisscrossed the Caribbean Sea, Caribbean and North American cultures have acknowledged each other. Though some cultural nationalists within the Caribbean may speak in emotional terms about American cultural penetration of the region, especially through cable television, the fact is that Caribbean culture has by other means penetrated North America. Reggae as a category of the Grammy awards, and the numerous Carnivals testify to Caribbean cultural penetration of the United States. The point is that any objective assessment of cultural inter-action within the Americas has to acknowledge that notwithstanding the enormity of the differences in size, resources and power, the Caribbean has never been overwhelmed culturally and the exchanges have never been one-way. Indeed, in music, Caribbean popular culture has proven to be a competitor to American popular culture in the global marketplace. That it has not always reaped the financial and economic returns from its cultural products may have to do more with copyright laws, or the lack thereof, and dependence on marketing agencies outside of the region over which it exercises no control than either to creative energy or widespread appeal.

The ACS signals an intent to promote greater economic integration within the region. However, any assumption that there are substantial cultural connections and understanding that will make it both feasible and viable is somewhat optimistic and could rightly be regarded as a gross overstatement of the reality. Although it is true that there are existing ties through the commonalities in the material culture of the people in the region, much of this is still undiscovered by the vast majority of inhabitants of the Caribbean. Sports, especially football, athletics, and table tennis, represent the broadest areas of exchange, interchange, and contact. Even then the mechanisms of the organization of these sporting contacts are mainly located in the councils of the international bodies related to the professional levels of these sports. These do not represent grass-roots exchanges within the region.

If culture is interpreted in its narrow meaning as the performing and creative arts, probably the most indigenous instrument of cultural integration emerging in the Caribbean, as a whole, has been the Caribbean Festival of Arts. This was first mounted in Puerto Rico in 1952 and inaugurated as CARIFESTA in Guyana in 1972; and it has been held periodically since. The objectives of CARIFESTA have been to expose the people of the region to each other's culture through the celebration of the activities of the creative arts, to forge through cultural participation closer relations between the peoples of the region and to demonstrate the importance of the arts as a unifying force in developing society (Nettleford 1978).

Transportation between the four subregions of the Caribbean is indicative of the degree of routine contact between them. Within any language group, there is regular and routine contact. However, between language groups, with the exception of Cuba, the easiest means of travel is through Miami. It is through the bilateral routes between the United States and each language group that the region finds it easiest to travel among themselves.

The existing travel paradigm, within the Caribbean as defined by the ACS, highlights the cultural challenges posed to the new Association. The psyche and the soul of the Caribbean, shaped and fashioned by the same historical legacies and geographical contours, are fractured if not fragmented by its history and geography. It will require more than economic necessity to give the ACS regional meaning. In this regard there is no greater obstacle to hurdle than that of the cultural barriers beginning with language.

Having been conceived principally as an instrument of economic necessity, the ACS has declared its first order of business as stimulating Caribbean tourism internationally, and promoting interregional transportation and trade regionally. The extent to which regional economics can be successfully pursued without the growth of significant cultural interchange within the region is a major question. Indeed, language represents a major obstacle in some parts of the region. In this regard the Dutch Caribbean is definitely at an advantage, given their historic efforts to communicate with the rest of the region. The English-speaking Caribbean may be at the greatest disadvantage, given its embrace of the traditional English chauvinism towards learning other languages.

Real doubts exist as to the degree to which the ACS will be able to accomplish its economic objectives. As an economic and trading mechanism, it appears to some to be already dead in the water. Even if it is able to get off the ground, there is great reservation concerning its effectiveness, given the economic realities of the global marketplace.

The greatest longterm prospects offered by the ACS appear to be in the area of culture and not economics. The term culture is used here in its wider meaning, that of the way of life of the people encompassing shared meanings, habitual outlooks, routine relationships, and cherished values. The Caribbean is the geographical center of the Americas. However, currently it exists on the periphery of wealth, power, and status in the hemisphere. The ACS, by bringing into association the different cultural streams of the hemisphere, opens the prospect that one day they may flow into a single river. Taking the long view, it can be said that the countries of the Americas cannot forever continue to practice material cultures that are offshoots of the Old World, particularly Europe. They cannot forever look to the past for meaning, values, habits, and outlooks. Though it is necessary to reach backwards to conserve the best of the contributions of the ancestors, it is imperative to move forward, taking account of the dynamic forces at work in contemporary circumstances.

While drawing upon the rich heritage of Africa, Asia, and Europe, the peoples of the Americas must in time construct cultures that are based upon the imperatives of the New World. The creation of an American culture and civilization appears to be the destiny of the peoples who now permanently reside in this hemisphere.

The ACS poses the challenge of facing the issues of cultural amalgamation and transformation sooner rather than later. At least three tasks become immediately mandatory. To begin with, it requires that people master more than their local Creole and the official language of their country. Further, it requires the abandonment of the aura and assumptions of superiority/inferiority that the Europeans promoted with respect to their assessment and regard for African and Asian heritage. Also it requires that the peoples of the region construct their relationships based upon mutual respect.

UNITED STATES AND CARIBBEAN INTERACTIONS: OBSERVATIONS

Apart from coming to terms with its internal imperatives, the greatest challenge facing Caribbean states collectively through the ACS, and individually, is that of their relationship and interactions with the United States. As the first nation of the Americas, the founding fathers of the United States envisioned a new civilization premised on equality, freedom, and justice. In ascending the heights of imperial status, the United States has lost its way in the Americas as its pursuit of power and wealth has diminished its commitment to social and cultural ideals. The United States has been known to undermine democracy in the Caribbean in the name of national interest, something the founding fathers would no doubt have regarded as unforgivable.

The challenges posed by the United States emerge from a combination of five considerations:

1. As the first new nation of the New World, the United States championed the ideals of republicanism, democracy, and freedom and stood against monarchical forms of government, oligarchy, and aristocracy as the bases of societal organization. The crusading vision and the idealism of the nineteenth century has dimmed in the twentieth century as the United States has risen in global power and status. The early idealism has been reduced largely to rhetoric as national interests—as measured in terms of American security, lives, jobs, and corporations—have become the dominant criteria in assessing U.S. involvement beyond its borders.

2. The United States is the first country of the Americas to emerge as a superpower in the world. Currently it is the most dominant power in the world, militarily. In pursuing its quest for imperial power, the United States has concentrated its efforts outside the hemisphere, particularly in Europe, the Middle East, and Asia. Indeed, it is not unfair to say that until very recently with NAFTA, by and large the United States took this hemisphere for granted and regarded the Caribbean as not much more than its backyard to which it retreats for relaxation, particularly on its beaches. In fact, the greatest attention paid to the

Caribbean resulted from Russian intrusion in Cuba. Even now, the potential markets of China and other countries of the Far East hold more fascination for the United States than the so-called "banana republics" of the region. Global status combined with the inherited European assumptions of superiority and the American assertion of greatness conspire to produce an aura of condescension in U.S. perception and dealings with the rest of the hemisphere, and with the Caribbean in particular.

3. The United States has paid a high price for its present superpower status. Part of that price is reflected in the deficit of the federal budget. The repayment of this debt will of necessity impact negatively on the standard of living of ordinary citizens. The politics of this situation can be expected to heighten xenophobic tendencies in U.S. relations with other countries. American security, lives, jobs, corporations, and interests can be expected to be the bottom line with mere genuflection and rhetorical correctness being accorded to the well-being and welfare of other countries.

4. Given the wide differences in power and influence between the United States and Caribbean states, it is almost certain that negative trends within the United States will be magnified ten fold in their effect in the Caribbean. Within the hemisphere, if the U.S. economy sneezes, the Canadian economy catches a cold, the Latin American economies contract bronchitis, and Caribbean economies develop pneumonia. Illustrations of this order of magnitude of effect are the negative impact that free trade has had on the Canadian economy, compared to the devastation that will descend upon the economies of the Windward Islands as a result of the planned removal of preferential access to the European banana market that U.S. corporations have insisted upon, backed by U.S. government pressure on the European Union.

5. The ideological milieu in the United States is currently dominated by the New Right. Habermas (1985) asserted that what is common to the evaluative schema of the New Right critique of the contemporary situation in the several societies is their affirmative stance toward social modernity and denigration of cultural modernity. Broadly defined, social modernity seeks to apply technical innovations to solve social problems, to produce growth and prosperity; whereas cultural modernity, which embraces hedonism, self-actualization, and alternative lifestyles, seeks the extension of rights of individuals, equity, and justice, and the positive freedoms of association, communication, debate, and claiming new rights. New Right's position therefore is not only an

attack on licentiousness but also an assault on the exercise of individual rights and freedom in society (Elliott and MacLennan 1994).

The safety valve of the Caribbean, over the last 130 years, has been emigration. That door is now firmly closed to Europe, and the door to the United States is being similarly shut. Ironically, the current ideology is for the free movement of goods, services, and capital, as dictated by comparative advantage. At the same time, the policy is for people and labor to be confined behind immigration barriers. Clearly the simultaneous pursuit of these two sets of policies is both illogical and unjust. However, the countries advocating these policies, including the United States, have the power to enforce them. Given the power and influence of the United States, its concentration on global matters largely outside the hemisphere, its current preoccupation with national interests, and its political economy in the context of the federal deficit in contrast to the marginal status of Caribbean States, it is reasonable to expect that U.S.-Caribbean relations will be dominated by friendly and sophisticated prosecution of advantage with respect to U.S. interests combined with benign neglect where Caribbean interests are involved. It is almost assured that the rhetoric will be correct on all sides, while the reality will be asymmetric advantage in favor of a seemingly benevolent United States. In other words, the economic recession and social retrogression experienced by the Caribbean over the last decade are unlikely to be reversed in the immediate future.

U.S. interrelations with the Caribbean cannot be seen simply in economic terms. The dominance of New Right ideology, promoted through the mass media and other contacts with the region, should not be overlooked. Caribbean societies are culturally conservative, particularly with respect to licentiousness and alternative lifestyles. The general tendency is to regard these matters as personal choices that individuals are free to make in private but should not be condoned or promoted in the public sphere. Aspects of the New Right's assault on cultural modernity will therefore find some resonance with the Caribbean. However, the attack on equality and equity, individual rights, and freedom and the assertion of the superiority of Western culture with the implied denigration of other cultures will repel large segments of Caribbean populations from embracing New Right positions.

These are the broad parameters within which Caribbean States collectively and individually must embark upon fundamental changes in both their regional and national cultures. In other words, it is within the context of projected adversity, continued marginality, U.S. opposition to the ACS, and an ideological orientation within the United States with ambiguous elements in relation to Caribbean realities that the region must find the political courage and the moral resources to reconfigure itself and reconstruct its culture as it proposes to become the cultural and ideological center of the Americas. Though the stimulus to form the ACS may be economic, its real mission is to reconfigure the region so that the heart and core of its current structure, culture, and civilization are transformed.

Assaulting what Mills (1993) refers to as the unholy trinity of race, class, and gender is an issue of preeminent importance in any attempt to transform Caribbean society and culture. Those who predicted the declining significance of race were both unduly optimistic and somewhat premature. Ethnic cleansing in Europe, the reversal of several of the gains of the Civil Rights movement in the United States and the resurgence of racism generally pose considerable challenges to the Caribbean where racial integration has progressed furthest in the world. The challenge to the Caribbean is to proceed with the completion of a process from which much of the rest of the world seems to be retreating. Indeed, the Caribbean has no other viable option, because to imitate global trends would be to negate its indigenous imperative as well as to undermine and subvert social peace in the region.

Reference has already been made to the fact that outside of Africa, the Caribbean is the only region in the world where people of African ancestry constitute the numerical majority in several countries. In the context of resurgence in racism and the current state of affairs in Africa, particularly in Nigeria, it is imperative that Caribbean nations, and the region as a whole, assume leadership in demonstrating the principles and practices of racial equality, the obvious fact of the common humanity of all people, and the potential of cultural diversity in enhancing and enriching the quality of life of peoples, nations, and regions.

Accordingly, developments within the Caribbean over the next decade will be of global importance. Within North America at least three constituencies should have particular interest in the course of social and cultural transformation within and between Caribbean societies: Caribbean nationals and people of Caribbean ancestry living in North America, the African-American community generally, and those members of the wider American society committed to the cannons of multiculturalism and the principle of racial equality as organizing criteria within society.

The interest in this mission and agenda cannot simply be that of the spectator or the academic. More than information and reflection is required. The fact is that what happens in the Caribbean in all likelihood will have material implications for the three groups named. More than that, because these three named groups are located in the United States, there is the distinct possibility that their involvement and engagement with Caribbean issues could make substantial differences to the outcomes.

The essence of the point being made here is this. The dominant minorities in the Caribbean have maintained their hegemony over the marginal majority largely with external assistance without which their hold on the society would be short-lived. The circumstances of the middle decades of the present century favored fundamental change in the region. However, the situation at the end of the century in terms of economic recession and structural adjustment has favored the status quo. Those supportive of and in solidarity with the interests of the marginal majority must become intimately involved to help balance the forces aligned against them.

It must be immediately stated that one is not here engaging in advocacy for financial aid or development assistance for the Caribbean or the marginal majorities in the various countries. The issue at hand is not finance but ideals, not handouts and benefits but principles and justice. To turn it around, one is not here speaking about the ways in which the interests of the United States can be promoted and prosecuted in the Caribbean in terms of jobs, corporations, and colleges but rather how American ideals can be fostered, where America is understood to mean the hemisphere and the ideals are those first enunciated by the founding fathers of the United States dealing with the virtues of equality, justice, worth, and dignity.

It must be noted that the founding fathers of the United States, through the Declaration of Independence and the Constitution, espoused the establishment of society and culture in the Americas on the cornerstones of freedom and equality. If one ignores as distractions the fact that the founding fathers engaged in practices and lived lives that were not consistent with the principles they expounded, the fact is that they established in the highest instruments of law the principles by which the inconsistencies of their lives could be ultimately resolved. For that they deserve credit. At the same time, it must be observed that some generations of their descendants have not proved worthy of their legacy and have reneged upon the lofty ideals of their ancestors. Indeed, the current generation seems to have turned the noble vision of a just society into a materialistic dream that can be fulfilled more in the lottery than by business acumen and hard work.

CHALLENGES WITHIN THE CARIBBEAN

Within the Caribbean the challenges in transforming the culture of nations and the region will reside around four principal elements:

1. Mobilizing people to become involved with the fundamental transformation of ordinary relationships codified and routinized in the paradigms of the past. For example, the transformation of man-woman relationships so that they are based on personhood and not patriarchy; relationships with children expanded outside the norms of the privatized nuclear family and incorporated within the norms of communal responsibility; and relating across the differences of race, class, and gender without assumptions of superiority or inferiority.

2. Promoting the learning and mastery of other peoples' languages and cultures as the basis of social interaction based upon mutual respect. At a minimum this should translate into the learning of English, French, Spanish, and the local Creole, the language of the soul of the people.

3. Mastering and mobilizing modern communication technology and deploying it as a means of nurturing, fostering, and promoting regional integration. Modern communication technology offers a unique capacity that can help to mitigate some of the limitation imposed by the geography of the region.

4. Linking the educational institutions within the region, commencing with colleges and universities, so that integration is sustained in the long term. Learning and leaders are key elements in creating and maintaining cultural contact and intercourse.

CONCLUDING COMMENT

Caribbean transformation at the end of the twentieth century demands affirmation not retreat, hope not despair, boldness not timidity, belief not doubt, and above all faith and confidence in its capacity to fashion its future. In the end it is service, sacrifice, and solidarity that will allow men and women of the region to fashion a civilization premised on personhood not gender, on the common humanity of all people not race and class, on justice not injustice, and on love not hate.

Fundamental change begins in the margin. Marginalized people within the region have a glorious opportunity to embark on radical and fundamental change directed at the very core of society and heart of civilization. To understand the mission in lesser terms is not to take the Caribbean seriously, and to miss the opportunities of the new millennium is to squander it potentials.

REFERENCES

Elliott, Brian, and David MacLennan. 1994. "Education, Modernity and Neo-Conservative School Reform in Canada, Britain and the United States," *British Journal of Sociology of Education*. Volume 15, No. 2, 1994. pp. 165–85.

Habermas, J. 1985. "Neo-Conservative Culture Criticism in the United States and Germany: An Intellectual Movement in Political Cultures." in R. Berstein, (ed.), *Habermas and Modernity*. Cambridge, Mass: MIT Press.

Mills, Charles W. 1993. "A Comment on Race, Class and Gender—The Unholy Trinity." In J. Edward Greene, (ed.), *Race, Class and Gender in the Future of the Caribbean*. Kingston: Institute of Social and Economic Research, University of the West Indies, Mona. pp. 111–14.

Nettleford, Rex M. 1978. *Caribbean Cultural Identity: The Case of Jamaica, An Essay in Cultural Dynamics*. Kingston: Institute of Jamaica.

Palacio, Joseph O. 1990. *Socioeconomic Integration of Central American Immigrants in Belize*. Mexico City: Published for Spear by Cubola Productions.

Smith, M. G. 1965. *The Plural Society in the West Indies*. Berkeley and Los Angeles: University of California Press.

Smith, Raymond T. 1967. "Social Stratification, Cultural Pluralism and Integration in West Indian Societies." In Sybil Lewis and Thomas G. Matthews, (eds.), *Caribbean Integration: Papers on Social, Political and Economic Integration*. Rio Piedras, Puerto Rico: Institute of Caribbean Studies, pp. 226–58.

8

Channels of Discovery: Perceptions of Culture and Sovereignty in the Caribbean

Merle Collins

As I was constructing my ideas for this chapter, I found myself asking, whom do I want to share these ideas with and to what end? Perhaps I found some clues in the idea that this is meant to prepare African-American and other minorities to participate in the formulation and implementation of U.S. foreign policy. So the question becomes what practical good to the Caribbean is a paper, so far from the Caribbean ethos? Of what practical good is it to Caribbean people living abroad? Because there are lots of Caribbean people around, discussions like these could move us closer to an understanding of our contradictions and move U.S. policymakers closer to an understanding of the issues that inform our exchanges.

But then to whom is this important? Can these largely small island nations have any impact on the shaping of policy? In the Cold War days, perhaps it was possible to have some moments of doubtful glory in the spotlight by talking about self-determination, not being in anybody's backyard (anybody meaning the United States), and causing policymakers to sit up and take notice of whose backyard you might in that case be drifting into. That was clearly a sketchy profile of the responses of and to the Bishop government in Grenada between 1979 and 1983 and to a long-ago, now mythical sounding Guyana government of the 1950s, and even to a one-time

Manley government in Jamaica. Now that there appears to be no other ideological backyard from which to save most of the Caribbean nations, some of them banana-oriented without having the distinction of being republics—one like Grenada, having in abundance an exotic product like nutmegs and spices and having little international bargaining power—where do we go from here?

As long as we Caribbean people keep quiet about our existence, it is easy—and perhaps even politic—for the United States to appear to do so also until some other cold war scenario or its equivalent threatens. This, too, is a cultural matter. Cultural expression and attitudes to Caribbean culture are intimately bound up with the question of politics.

The idea of culture and sovereignty, referred to in the title of this paper, suggests something to preserve, suggests a nation's right to exercise exclusive autonomy over its own traditions and customs and to ensure, perhaps, that the cultures (ideas, values) of other nations do not become more important than its own in the shaping of its sense of self. One might well ask, why not? And if we consider the case of a Jamaica, we might even say, well, Louise Bennett is respected enough, quite a few individuals there have a sense that research into cultural customs is important, and there is a great deal recorded on video. Sistren Theatre Collective has international recognition; further to the south in the Caribbean, calypso is known internationally, even if it doesn't have quite the international profile of reggae, except during Carnival, when Caribbean communities abroad help to internationalize it. But let us look at more than these theatrical manifestations of culture, or even perhaps consider how and when the recognition is acquired.

People comment about ubiquitous American television in the region. The soaps *The Young and the Restless, The Bold and the Beautiful,* and *As the World Turns* are particularly popular. And we might pay some attention to the lyrics of one St. Lucian calypsonian, Ashanti—lyrics innovative at least in its general ethos: "As the world turns, bold and beautiful, the young getting restless" (Banyan Films 1992). One might well ask, is any harm done? But these soaps, and other American programs, sell a particular version of the American dream and contribute to the creation of expectations that can only be met by the outflow of both money and people. Those who doubt this have only to consider the fact that lots of money is spent in this country on advertising, because it is perceived to bring results; those advertisements are part of the Caribbean diet, if only because programs sometimes come complete with their commercial breaks. Advertisements come, too, complete with their 1–800 number to be dialed, even if this can't be reached from the particular Caribbean country. So the Caribbean is part of the market for American goods and services, and American culture helps to sell America.

A Caribbean film, Banyan Production for a BBC program on Developing Studies, did a comparative analysis of television programming in St. Lucia and Cuba. This is instructive because it shows something of the unease of cultural workers and other intellectuals with the present state of programming in many Caribbean countries (the film was produced in 1992) and also indicates what was held out as an alternative model of operation then, instructive because little has changed where television programming is concerned, even if a great deal has changed in terms of the political map and ideological divisions. There continues to be dissatisfaction, and somewhere along the line there may be radical attempts at change. The more dissatisfied one becomes with the existing state of things, the more likely it is that change will be radical, or even, some might assess, extreme. In the Banyan film, Keats Compton, the manager of Cable and Wireless, St. Lucia, explained in an interview that there were 16 channels in their system. Four of those were local and regional—two St. Lucian, two others from Barbados and Martinique—the other twelve were satellite delivered from the United States direct, with satellite dishes. And even the two so-called local channels had about 90 percent foreign content. The Cable and Wireless official was conscious, he said, of television's influence on the local population's image of itself. It was, however, a business decision; the viewers wanted it. One individual, Clem Bobb, operated a community television station from his home. In additon to the local community material, he also used some satellite material but prerecorded it to ensure that the advertisements were removed. This was because of his perception that they affected consumerism patterns. For example, he said, arrowroot was produced in the area. Why have commercials that developed a taste for cornflakes? On that very basic, local level, Bobb was showing something of the importance of the cultural product to the shaping of demand and supply patterns, to the use of currency. The film pointed out that St. Lucia, with roughly 150,000 people, an income per capita of U.S. $2000, had 17 channels with a total of less than 5 percent local content. Well, as one interviewee said, "The licenses to operate come from the government and if the government doesn't like it, you'd soon hear about it." Against this was juxtaposed the case of Cuba, with 10.5 million people, 3 television channels, local program content of 70 percent, and of the United States, with a population 247 million, (income per capita $20,000), over 100 TV channels, local program content, 99 percent. The filmmakers interviewed Antonio Navarro, Director of Broadcasting at Radio Marti/T.V. Marti. Navarro spoke about the restrictions of Cuban television, the Castro government's control of programming, the determination of T.V. Marti to continue its programming in spite of jammed signals that made beaming to Havana difficult. It was important, he said, as a thorn in the side of the government. And he added, "Besides, we're only talking about 18 million dollars; a tank in a war costs significantly more than that, or an aeroplane, or a single missile." And one who knows the difference $18 milion could make to the budget of any Caribbean country could only reflect ruefully on the cost of what is perhaps regarded as cure, and reflect ruefully also on the economic differences that continue to affect production and absorption of the cultural product.

The Banyan production suggests that some cultural workers in the Caribbean are concerned with preservation of a sense of self. In an effort to do something about a situation where CNN weather news concentrates on dense fog while they sit in brilliant sunshine, cultural workers look for other models and think also of the means to develop local attractive programming to cater to various tastes. For the focus can't simply be on removing expatriate programming but also on developing local programming that would satisfactorily replace foreign images. And in this discussion, every Caribbean person's image of self is important. I explain this last by saying that I am reminded of a statement by Merle Hodge of Trinidad on the subject of art and activism. Referring specifically to Caribbean literature, Merle Hodge wrote, "We are occupied by foreign fiction." She adds that "merely to portray Caribbean experience with the power of art is to pluck this experience out of limbo and give it a distinct shape and a name. I am not talking about idealizing Caribbean reality. Literature contributes to a people's growth by portraying them both respectfully and critically, not by flattering them" (Cudjoe 1990). On the general subject of culture, "the full spectrum of responses that a people makes, collectively, to its specific environment, to ensure its survival in that environment," that, Hodge says, is yet to be properly addressed in a Caribbean context. She notes that television, essentially American television, came to Trinidad and Tobago in 1962, the year the British flag was pulled down and Trinidad became that elusive thing called independent.

In spite of the fact that the Caribbean people continue to create a vibrant culture everyday, wherever we live, mediated by circumstances wherever we are, this culture—not just the Carnival and performance arts elements of it, but everthing that contributes to the psychological makeup of Caribbean people—is not highly valued. And in discussing this, perhaps I am invoking the link between culture and development, between colonialism (new or old) and radical attempts at change (see, for example, Said 1993). The attempt at revolutionary change in Grenada 1979, for example, did not just come from nowhere. It was created and shaped by the story of the country and the region—political, economic, social, including all of the things that make up a people's culture—and in the end, affected by people's responses to U.S. intervention.

Not only do Caribbean people working in the United States send remittances to friends and relatives in the region but considerable sums are spent in the United States by Caribbean people purchasing food and clothing for relatives in the Caribbean. And these kinds of connections, valued by people in the region, contribute a great deal to the shaping of public opinion regarding the United States. These unstructured business and social relationships help to shape pro-American political attitudes among many people and contribute to the sympathy towards the United States, which, for political reasons and to sell the cause of invasion, was so often remarked upon, for example, in the days following the U.S. invasion of Grenada. In a post-Independence situation where neocolonial economies are very fragile, the strength of the U.S. economy remains a potent attraction.

This sociopolitical relationship has a great deal to do with culture. What is the Channels of Discovery in the title of this chapter? Shortly after the October 1983 U.S. invasion of Grenada, a U.S. psychological operations unit set to work removing billboards and doing other things to erase physical signs of the Bishop regime; not so much erasing the memory of the brutal murders of October 19 but of everything to do with the regime. There also appeared on television a channel called Discovery Channel, and for a while the television station was known as Discovery Television. Now it's largely a question of context. Discovery Channel may be quite harmless as part of the general U.S. fare; in the particular Grenada situation, with its colonial history and such recent vaunting of notions of anticolonialism, Discovery Television seemed to be sending signals about a new colonialism.

Having thrown in this idea of discovery, perhaps plausible in the Reagan era, let me go back to that earlier idea of local culture. First, the question of language. Increasingly, Caribbean researchers such as Hubert Devonish, Morgan Dalphinis, and others are researchng Creoles and establishing a place for what we have come to call Caribbean dialects as viable Creole languages. There is a Cassidy dictionary of Jamaican Creole. Richard Allsopp's Dictionary of Caribbean usage was recently published (1996). Throughout the region, in Trinidad, Barbados, St. Lucia, and Grenada, research is being done on language issues, and people are interested in tracing the history of language formulations and the construction of Creoles from African languages such as Wolof, Yoruba, Gaa, and others, from Hindi, English, Spanish, Dutch, etc. So far this has had more impact in the academic institutions than in the average community. Because these issues are being confronted in countries with little international economic or political power, it is an uphill struggle to have changing perceptions about language translate into any significant empowerment where the attitude to the cultures is concerned. Those who can move with relative facility between the use of English or French or some other European language and a Creole can more comfortably discuss these issues. Those for whom Creole is their major (perhaps only) language are usually more conscious of language difference and perhaps more likely to feel a sense of inadequacy in a forum where English or French or one of the official (even if not majority) languages is being used. So when we come to study Caribbean languages in the classroom, parents are naturally cautious about the ideas being passed on there. If it is true that language is the only homeland, then a lot of us Caribbean people, when interacting with the world, are very uneasy about this homeland, perhaps because of what is considered to be perceptions of its international socioeconomic status.

Now the use of Creole language forms on the stage is a different thing—in theater, in poetry readings—understandable, acceptable, enjoyable in that forum; but in official communication, in the writing of this paper, not the norm. Regarding the teaching of Caribbean literature—from my experience of teaching in England and now here in the United States, I will say that there is a thirst among literature students of Caribbean origin, in this case born in the United States of Caribbean parents, or born there and moved here perhaps at an early age, to know something of the region. A literature course often includes something of a course on the history and culture of the region, so that students understand something of the background for development of the particular work. This interest is also there among other students (and here many African-American students) who want to know more about the region that is so close to them and of whose existence they know little beyond their attractiveness as possible tourist destinations. As a result of the colonial experience, Caribbean writers appear to me to be much better known in London than they are in the Washington area. It seems to me that this is one way, exploring the fiction and the links between literature and history, that the United States could better inform itself about a region that, because of its very proximity (its position there in the Caribbean sea), is of importance to the United States. And as I mention what is of the strategic importance so much talked about during the Reagan 1992 period, I would just like to spend a few minutes making a point or two about ideology, meaning really the realm of ideas.

It is one of the stranger results of Caribbean political dissent that those involved, when they flee their countries, seek refuge in places such as the United States or Britain or Canada, even when the governments they may have been opposing at home have been seeking or receiving tacit or other support from those very countries. Now it seems to me that one of the things that this points to is how size influences attitudes to political debate. Here in the United States, an individual might say something at the International Affairs Center and most of the rest of Washington really doesn't know what's going on; now if this meeting is taking place in Grenada or St. Lucia or St. Vincent or Trinidad, many (perhaps even most) people know something about it, and if anyone makes a remark that seems to be critical of government, various versions of the story get noised abroad pretty quickly. This has an impact on perceptions. Because of the size of our countries, intellectual debate is often a question of taking sides; in cases where, for example, it is perceived that pronouncements might affect the tourist industry or the U.S. attitude, or foreign perceptions, or might seem to be an attack on a particular family position, problems are intensified. These are not only neocolonial constructs but also, or perhaps and therefore, the sensitivity of vulnerable economies conscious of how economic and political power may be wielded against them. And perhaps it is also true that the intellectuals, who outside of office seem to have a sense of vision, can quickly get stumped by the everyday business of government, dealing with the petty, huge details regarding the Caribbean Development Bank, and the nutmeg shipments, and the World Bank meeting, and details about bananas, wondering who to send to the U.N. meeting, and all of those necessary details which are so time-consuming. It is like being at the University or in some other office and putting off the grand, visionary projects because of the tiny, constricting day-to-day details that clutter the desk.

And how does all of this link in with the notion of cultural pride and television programming and psychological operations units? Now following the invasion of Grenada, a plaque honoring the Americans who died defending Grenada was placed outside the international airport. But there is no equivalent symbol for the Grenadians who died, many of them not even involved in the battle—not, that is, actively engaged in supporting one side or the other. People who were there, for example, at the fort on the day that Bishop and others were murdered; those who jumped off the fort; no local commemoration to a traumatic time and to the national pain that an apparent search for what was described during those years as self-esteem could end in such tragedy; yes, there were mistakes; yes, there were violations of individual rights; yes, there was cause to mourn; but this was a time when Grenada came close to knowing itself, knowing the contradictory notions that inform its existence, when there was a sense of vision gone awry. How can there be a tribute to the Americans and not one other significant local monument to that tragic time for all Grenadians? Now I raise this not by way of critiquing any particular Grenada government. Perhaps the idea would not be a popular one, and governments are wary of opposition. I am simply noting the kinds of self-effacement that can occur when a culture has its sense of self consistently eroded. Admittedly, it is still a difficult subject for Grenada, traumatized as it was by the brutal events of those days. But sometimes using the culture as far as possible to re-create the history is itself a healing. I think of such things when I sit on a train in London, for example, and look up at an advertisement that advises me, below a picture of Henry VIII, to take the train to The Tower and take in an execution before dinner; or when I look at programs about Jack the Ripper, or the Profumo Scandal, or, closer to here and nearer in time, the Iran-Contra Affair, on the C.I.A. in Nicaragua, on Nixon. Somehow, when in the Caribbean there are political events that are considered unpalatable, discussing them is fraught with dangers and it would seem that this has to do with more than the uncomfortable restrictions imposed by size. I would concede that it is certainly partly the politics of size; but it is, I think, also the culture developed by a constant exaggerated care engendered by a sense of socioeconomic and political vulnerability. Be careful what you say, some big country might not like it; and this kind of inheritance stifles cultural debate, makes intellectuals more timid in their own countries than they are outside of it, even if attitudes in foreign countries may also encourage timidity.

And even as we ponder these issues, considering how it might be possible to influence U.S. policy towards the region, it is important to recognize that all of this contributes to an unequal relationship with a country like the United States. Some questions to consider: Are they mainly intended to help the United States to know the Caribbean better? To what end? To contribute in some way, possibly, to the shaping of policy? And perhaps the fundamental question is, where a subject like culture is concerned, what are the U.S. policies that would be of benefit to the Caribbean? Would they at the same time be of benefit to the Caribbean? Is it important to juggle a sense of cultural pride with a sense of economic neces-sity? And, where culture is concerned, it is perhaps important to recognize that the United States like the Caribbean, does not have a monolithic culture. Perhaps it is important for the Caribbean in the United States to temper the possiblity of insular Caribbean-ness with the recognition that there is a sibling constituency among African-Americans, with the understanding that there are many shared perceptions, shared interests; that many African-Ameri-cans, if we trace the history and the literature (history with the small *h* and with the big *H*) way back, were Caribbean people; that there is the shared link of all being Africans in the Americas; that there are also Asiatic Caribbean people and Asiatic North Ameri-cans; that the socioeconomic and political status of the Caribbean as a region is shared by many individual African-Americans.

This understanding of the history to help shape perceptions of the culture and to help make dynamic a Caribbean culture abroad is about politics, is about economics, is about culture. When I study in the archives of places like here in the United States, even when the material is in the Library of Congress (and the Grenada docu-ments housed there give evidence to a new colonialism), or in the Public Records Office in London, however much I may regret the fact that so much of my history is housed in these places outside of the country, I am struck by the respect that is paid to documen-tation, by the impeccable condition in which documents are kept, and by the organization that ensures that this condition continues. And then I go to archives in some Caribbean countries. In one case recently, records that I used only eight years ago were no longer available. I was told that they were in too fragile a condition to be handled; remembering the state they were in when I used them previously, I was not surprised. Is this because of economics? because the Caribbean countries culturally seem to have little interest in or notion of the type of competition that engenders development of the capitalist economy? I am told that records housed in various places in Barbados, however, are in quite good condition; in a condition not unlike that in which records are kept at the PRO in London. Why, then? If not economics, or at least not only economics, is it because of the value that is placed on material that records the history and culture of the nation? This is an issue not for the United States but for Caribbean people abroad as we consider the shaping of priorities, as we consider projects that we might influence.

When I go to museums in various countries today, I remember the experience, when I was at High School in Grenada, of going on archaeological digs with visiting expatriates, being excited at recovering for them bits of pottery (Carib pottery, I was told), handing these over, and being pleased about the praise. Where are these things today, I wonder? Is this still happening in parts of the region? Are there parts of our cultural and historical stories hidden in various parts of the universe that we need to claim, if, that is, we can use the vision to preserve them properly? When I think of issues such as this, I find it difficult to determine the importance of discussing culture in a manner intended to influence U.S. policymaking. Perhaps the importance is to influence the attitudes of Caribbean people in the area, to contribute in some way to a development of that self-awareness that would contribute to perspectives on lobbying for attention to Caribbean interests. Is the United States interested in issues such as those that I have mentioned? Should it be? If it is, from what perspective? And even if it isn't, don't we, Caribbean governments and people, have to be interested for our very understanding of our countries and our existence, regardless of where we are in the universe?

I conclude with a quotation from Merle Hodge. "Fiction (and perhaps all art) casts a redeeming and enhancing light back upon the reality from which it springs, endowing it with meaning, credibility, and authority. It allows a people not only to know its own world but to take it seriously" (Cudjoe 1990, 206). Taking oneself seriously can only contribute to the stability that is so often spoken of as being important for regional security and advancement.

REFERENCES

Banyan Films. 1992. *And the Dish Ran Away with the Spoon.*

Cudjoe, Selwyn. *Caribbean Women Writers,* Wellesley, MA: Calaloux Publications, 1990.

Said, Edward. *Culture and Imperialism,* Vintage Books, 1993.

9

Religious Imperatives in Caribbean Development: The U.S. Connection

Kortright Davis

There can hardly be any doubt today that the Caribbean region has been regarded by some people as the backyard of the United States—islands floating like objects in the great American lake, and specks of concern in the Old Basin. Dalton Narine has suggested that, "for most Americans, the image of the Caribbean is one of picturesque, sun-washed beaches, gently swaying palm trees, and gentle people greeting tourists with a smile. The Caribbean is all that, but it is also a vital political, economic and cultural part of the Western Hemisphere."[1] It holds together, in a very special way, islands of poverty and potential, groupings of revolt and survival, feelings of passion and anomie, germs of pleasure and pain, and bastions of pride and failure.

The region that embraces so many varieties of cultural expressions is still home to millions of people. The geopolitical factors that have dominated the entire history of the region have left their indelible mark on the social fabric of all its people. No sector can dare claim immunity from coming to terms with the proximity of the United States and all that this stands for.

It is only as we begin to look at Caribbean historical realities from the standpoint of the present back into the past that we can more effectively attempt an intelligent assessment of the complex nature of the communities we are discussing here and thus discern the movements for change that are currently on the way. The old Europe has virtually given way to the new Europe (United States of America), and the burden of survival in Caribbean existence is characterized by the common struggle of dealing with the presence of the latter-day forces of neocolonialism. The fact that there is yet no regional consensus on this common struggle lies close to the root of the complexity of Caribbean existence today and gives real meaning to the Caribbean reluctance to exchange one set of masters for another. This is the crucible in which the role of religion in the process of Caribbean development is best understood.

THE CARIBBEAN REGION

It is impossible to understand the nature of social change in the Caribbean as a whole without acknowledging the fact that the region still struggles to emerge from the shadow of the plantation. Apart from the nineteenth century independence movements beginning with Haiti in 1804, the moves towards independence that began in the 1960s did not usher in any radical changes of fortune, status, or power. New nations were born indeed, but the people were still not free. Political sovereignty came to mean nothing more than the transfer of authority from outside the region to the inside. Economic and cultural sovereignty were still to be defined and assumed.

The last three decades of Caribbean history have been characterized by a wide range of political experiments, all in search of asserting the meaning of freedom and independence in one form or other. Neocolonialism now reigns where once colonialism held sway. Formal political independence, in almost every aspect of Caribbean life, has been gravely affected by new layers of dependence, as a result of which certain factors still remain evident throughout the region.

First, the transition from plantations to societies is still on the way and has proven to be far more difficult than what the transfer of local authority would have suggested. Transnational corporations, offshore banking, foreign- or locally-owned hotels, and the globalization of the media have all retarded the extinction of the plantation and its mentality in the Caribbean. Secondly, the Caribbean is an open region, with no curtains to be drawn, no borders to be policed, and no political system to fix in place. The fact of Caribbean openness must never be lost sight of, for it was this that provided the Europeans with such a matchless opportunity for survival and expansion in the sixteenth and seventeenth centuries. In the Caribbean there is just too much sea and too little land.

Thirdly, the real ownership of the Caribbean as a whole is still very much in doubt culturally, economically, and ideologically. The fourth factor has to do with external linkages. For as it was with the earlier history of the region, when trade was central to its modern genesis, so too its current livelihood depends on its attachments to the outside world. Because of their declining ability to provide the necessary goods and services, the nature of these attachments takes on greater significance, for standards of living and levels of expectation fight to remain very much in place. Political fortunes are therefore very closely linked with political promises for better contacts with the outside world, especially the United States.

The fifth consideration relates to the Caribbean Diaspora, the people of Caribbean origin scattered across the globe in search of progress and survival. It is inherent in the Caribbean condition that the islands have not been able to give bread to all to whom they have given birth. The Caribbean Diaspora is thus an indispensable segment of Caribbean society, and no serious study of the region can be undertaken without due attention being paid to them.

In addition to these realities of dependence that we have been describing, the Caribbean remains a relatively poor region, with levels of poverty increasing all the time. Generally speaking, appearances of material growth and general social improvements are not matched by a substantial capacity to sustain them. There is therefore a pervasive form of disguised poverty in the region, so that "what you see is not really what you get." Disguised poverty is allied with some residual forms of cultural alienation. This pattern is not always easy to discern these days, as there is now a general aura and pervasive rhetoric of cultural self-determination and a popular social thrust to assert a local cultural identity.

Alienation, of course, breeds fragmentation, as if the region did not have enough of that already, with the scattered nature of its geography. Efforts at social, economic, political, and cultural integration between the islands have not always been blessed with success.

The Caribbean then is beset by endemic and persistent problems of dependence, poverty, alienation, and fragmentation. Yet this is not the whole picture, for the people as a whole continue to live out their existence with a number of distinctive virtues and characteristics, without which no progress would have been possible.

The common character of the Caribbean region has an obvious impact on the people who actually live there. They are endowed with a spirit of openness, which works for them most of the time but also hinders them some of the time. Caribbean people are known for their versatility, and this is evident by their mastery in a wide range of fields, their individual interests, and their adaptability. They are a very creative people, and this native creativity produces a broad range of celebrative styles and cultural habits. These give Caribbean people a very distinctive character and color in the mosaic of the global family. Further, they have had to develop skills for survival, acquiring the art of making a little go a long way and struggling against great odds such as hurricanes, drought, resource scarcity, underdeveloped social amenities, and dysfunctional technologies. Caribbean people are a hardy people; yet their humanity shines through with a radiance that is often infectious. Caribbean people have a way of making a significant difference in the places where they mix with persons of other cultures. The annual spectacle of Carnival in different parts of North America and Europe, the pervasive nature of reggae and calypso music all give testimony to this fact.

Caribbean music is much more than music; it is Caribbean life itself. No one who seeks to understand the strength of Caribbean life can ignore this important dimension of music, for it is deeply rooted in the soul of the people. It sustains them in their darkest moments, it gives them a sense of solidarity and worth, it nourishes the expression of their hopes and beliefs, it enkindles their spirits in the face of daunting material realities, it nurtures their young and gives marrow to the bones of their skeletal existence, it expresses their finest creative abilities as it interprets their innermost feelings, and it infects their environment with a force of cultural contagion that is almost irresistible. It liberates them from despair and from pretensions of superiority and intimidation. It sweetens the fabric of physical work, reinforces social upliftment, and energizes the practice of spiritual worship. Music, to be sure, is the Caribbean voice of God.[2]

Caribbean people, then, are incurably religious; and there is hardly a dichotomy between the sacred and secular. They are marked by these common religious characteristics:

- The world belongs to God and to no one else.
- Human life is somehow more sacred than it often appears.
- Human freedom is a basic divine right and not just a human privilege.
- God is unconditionally on the side of the poor and oppressed.
- "God don' love ugly."
- "Tief from tief mek God laugh."

Regardless of their religious persuasion, Caribbean people appear to share these principles in common. This is why it is impossible to examine the course and meaning of Caribbean social change without paying particular attention to the role of religion in that total process.

RELIGION AND CARIBBEAN CHANGE

The Caribbean story shows that the people themselves have often made great strides in struggling for emancipation through the creative use of their own religious expressions and experiences. Religion in the Caribbean has traditionally run along two parallel lines. First, there are the formally established churches of the Christian persuasion, and the various groupings within Islam, Hinduism, and Judaism. The second line consists of the indigenous religions that owe their genesis to their African religious heritage. Shango, Voudun, Rastafari, Cumina, Santeria and other religious expressions all play an important role in the development of Caribbean social life.

Apart from Voudun and Santeria, these indigenous religions are not as widespread as the established religions, nor do they enjoy the prominence or social status that they really deserve. They tend to provide for their adherents a strong sense of belonging and a mode of interpreting their environment and the realities of their condition. They generally tend to provide a sense of support for coping with the pressures of life rather than to create for them a major impetus for changing those realities. It may even be said that they sometimes induce a form of benign escape from the harsh realities of the social conditions.

The story of the Christian churches in the region begins with the settlement of the planter classes and their search for divine sanction for their way of life in the New World. Christianity took up its first position as a chaplaincy to the plantocracy. The churches were comprised at this time of planters who owned human chattel for work on their plantations; they worshipped their God and brutalized their slaves at the same time. This is simply because they claimed that their slaves had no souls to be saved. Nevertheless, apart from their traditional religious functions, the historic role of the churches in the field of education throughout the region cannot be denied or ignored.

In the course of time, the very churches that retained vestiges of colonial domination and dependence eventually began to throw off much of these burdens and to assume a radically different role in the transformation of society. It was basically from the 1960s and onwards, therefore, that we began to recognize radical social changes in the Caribbean, starting principally with the churches themselves. For not only did they assume the greater role of being a carrier and critique of the social conscience, at least at the level of their indigenous leadership, they also adopted the posture of becoming catalysts for social change and development. It is chiefly because the people in the Caribbean have assumed leadership and control of the churches in their area that such institutions have been able to be in the vanguard of social, cultural, political, and economic changes in the region. We can best assess their role within the categories of fragmentation, alienation, dependence, and poverty, to which we have earlier drawn attention.

We first need to review the general context in which such efforts for change are taking place. At least eight factors characterize the sociohistorical context for the churches' role in Caribbean development:

1. The withdrawal of the foreign missionaries from the region, or the decline in the authority of foreign mission boards.

2. The gradual improvement in the educational standards and achievements of the general population.
3. The gaining of political independence by most of the territories, accompanied by a stronger sense of control over social institutions.
4. The rise in nationalism and collective self-determination.
5. The advancements in indigenization of leadership, personnel, and customs throughout the region.
6. The common acceptance of a socio-cultural revolution and its implications for change in every aspect of social identity and religious practice.
7. The success of ecumenical movements within and without the region, and the patterns of solidarity which have been engendered.
8. The wave of global transformations throughout the Third World in particular and their impact on Caribbean life and thought.

All of these factors have had a most important impact on the course of social change in the region, and the interaction between church and society has been enormously significant in this context. It is the ecumenical movement in the Caribbean, however, that should mainly occupy our attention in what follows, because it has brought together more constituent churches than any other effort at social change or regional integration.

The Caribbean Conference of Churches was formally inaugurated in November 1973 in Kingston, Jamaica, when 16 of the mainline churches committed themselves to working together for radical change and development in the region and for purposeful renewal of their own structures.

This event had been preceded by the major Ecumenical Consultation on Development in Trinidad two years earlier (1971), when, at Chaguaramas, the churches joined with other regional bodies to work together for the political, economic, social, and cultural liberation of the Caribbean. Such liberation could not be realistic, they determined, without the full incorporation of Cuba into the mosaic of Caribbean relationships, regardless of what the Americans felt. Diplomatic relations with Cuba were established by many of the independent Commonwealth Caribbean countries shortly thereafter.

The decisions of the Chaguaramas Consultation were very far-reaching, for they created a significant shift in the kind of language and social revolution to which the churches were committing themselves for the first time in their history. Those decisions can be summarized as follows:

- The Caribbean should develop its own appropriate life-style.
- Caribbean people should participate fully in their own affairs.
- Development in the Caribbean required radical structural changes.
- The churches should be totally engaged in Caribbean development.
- Every effort should be made to work for Caribbean unity.

It was with this kind of working consensus within the churhes that the Caribbean Conference of Churches (CCC) found it possible to deploy its energies and resources towards movements for substantial change in the region. They committed themselves to four main objectives. These were:

1. "The promotion of a spirit of self-dependence by enlarging the people's capacity to generate and sustain indigenous development efforts."
2. "Providing catalysts for development efforts in the region."
3. "Making contributions to the material growth of the poorer people in the society."
4. "The promotion of the wider participation of the people in the social process and greater reconciliation among estranged groups in the society."

Through the establishment of many programs and its support of many projects, the CCC has been able to pioneer many initiatives in all of the Caribbean territories. It has been the main catalyst for bringing the local churches out of their passivity, whether in language or action, and it has been able to generate a wave of popular articulation and witness through a variety of communicative strategies. In summary terms, the CCC has tried to be consistent in exploring a variety of strategies that would seek to appropriate the meaning of the Gospel being preached in the churches to the structures and processes that affect the lives of their people. The creation of a general consensus in the Caribbean has been difficult, chiefly because of the predominance of adversarial politics and the rabid politics of personalism. Democratic institutions remain in place, but the participation of the people in the general processes still leaves much to be desired. There seem to be eight principal themes that are emerging in the ongoing path of social change in the region, and the churches have been very vocal in the articulation of these themes:

1. The promotion, affirmation and protection of basic Caribbean values.
2. The promotion of the Caribbean cultural spirit through education, sports, and the arts.
3. The generation of a wider entrepreneurial class and increased industrial aptitudes and appropriate technological proficiency.
4. The disciplined growth of the public sector as an agency for coordinating and stimulating private effort, and greater self-reliance.
5. The elimination of racism and class discrimination, as well as ethnic division.
6. The coordinated rationalization of relationships with the USA and its policies.
7. The reintegration of the Caribbean Diaspora into the life of the home territories.
8. The radical commitment to Caribbean self-determination with social and geopolitical implications.

These are the themes that seem to characterize much of the change to which the people of the Caribbean have been committed in recent times. How they have fared does not always make for a healthy story; but they have managed to address themselves in some way to what it means to struggle for emancipation and freedom.

CONCLUSION

The churches in the Caribbean, particularly through their collaborative efforts in the CCC, have attempted to pioneer a process of social change in the face of some endemic oppressive realities.

Nevertheless, the Church's fight against dependence is being waged by placing a heavy emphasis on self-reliance and the implications of political independence. The fight against poverty is being waged by stimulating efforts at creativity among the masses and by focusing attention on sustainable programs for economic growth and self-sufficiency. The fight against alienation is being waged by promoting programs of cultural liberation and affirmation, by pursuing the policies of indigenization in social institutions, and by stimulating popular demands for social justice, through common access and human rights. The fight against fragmentation is being waged by a struggling program of communication and community building at the grass-roots level. It has done more than any other regional grouping to build networks of regional solidarity and regional integration, and it has also complemented official efforts to penetrate the international community with a Caribbean presence.

The Caribbean remains locked into a vicious system of neocolonialism and strangled independence. Social change will therefore continue to mean a radical break with the past and a radical liberation of the mind, the values, the life-styles, and the patterns of relationships. The role of religion in all of this continues to be indispensable, for, at the very least, Caribbean people remain a deeply religious people, and the religious bodies continue to be the most powerful institutions in the region. Nevertheless, the power of these groups will not remain inviolate, for the rise of new generations with their crises of drug abuse, their imitation of American vices, the dissipation of cultural values, and political sectionalism will almost certainly wreak havoc if radical changes do not occur.

These words of William Demas should therefore continue to ring true: "The whole history of the Caribbean has been that of a long struggle for a place of dignity for the majority of the people in their own countries, for self-determination and for self-respect and the respect of others." Whatever the United States can do to further this process rather than to retard it will in the course of time extend the boundaries of its professed vision of global justice, social freedom, and the pursuit of happiness.

As for the full human development of Caribbean people themselves, eight religious imperatives are vital for their interests in the U.S.-Caribbean connection:

1. The recovery of the youth from their low expectations and misdirected sense of achievement.

2. The enrichment of Caribbean womanhood through principles of justice, equity, and empowerment.

3. The restabilization of home and family life through the redesignation of the extended family.

4. The "de-Anansitization" of Caribbean manhood towards greater levels of accountability.

5. The interchurch linkages between the home region and the Diaspora.

6. The creation of Caribbean sector lobbies in the extragovernmental and religious public advocacy groups in the United States.

7. The aggressive development and protection of Caribbean rules of taking and borrowing from external sources.

8. The promotion of more effective means of information delivery and public awareness of critically relevant issues at home and abroad.

Since the United States has benefitted so much more from the migration of Caribbean peoples than the Caribbean itself, it is time for the Caribbean to benefit much more from its U.S. connection. For every Caribbean Christian knows the irrevocable truth to the religious maxim, which also stands as an irrefutable imperative: God Helps Those Who Help Themselves. This is the central ethic and ethos of Caribbean development, which is still waiting to be fully discovered and fruitfully exploited.

NOTES

1. Dalton Narine, "The Changing Face of the Caribbean," *Ebony* (October 1988): 120.

2. Kortright Davis, *Emancipation Still Comin'* (New York:Orbis, 1990), p. 44.

Repositioning U.S.-Caribbean Relations: Reflections on Development and African-Caribbean-American Cultural Identities

James Early

With varying degrees of success, many historical attempts have been made to reposition Caribbean countries within "the region" as well as in relation to the United States and other countries in the Americas. What sensory symbols, language, and interpretive strategies are used to vivify the story(s) of historical and contemporary repositioning of U.S.-Caribbean relations are critical to understanding the complex dimensions of the subject. More so, the sources of consciousness or points of view (primary-lived and/or living class, racial, gender, and/or ethnic experiences) from which the narrative is derived are key to understanding the mode of presentation as well as to deciphering social and political meaning and new spatial implications of traditional terminology like "region" and "nation." For example, one critically important interpretation of more-recent attempts to reposition relations between the United States and the Caribbean, including the Caribbean Basin Initiative and the idea of an Association of Caribbean States (ACS), is that these periodic developments are objective reflections of transhistorical trends towards regionalization and globalization in commerce and communication, and interaction on all manner of mutual interests among nation-states. The terminology employed to convey dynamism and significance ("transhistorical," "globalization," "nation," etc.) reflects a coding system, a universe of discourse, and cultural valuation inhabited by economists, development specialists, political scientists, and cultural historians and theorists. Unfortunately, the social context from which this terminology is derived generally does not reflect the symbolic and expressive values and cultural behaviors of the diverse mass of inhabitants of the Caribbean region, notwithstanding their indispensable participation as workers and consumers in the transhistorical, globalizing developments.

The most distinguishing feature of present considerations in repositioning schemes, and arguably the most compelling historical motive leading to "repositioning" in many regions of the world, is global integration of nation-states and peoples into the world capitalist economy. Rapid, unprecedented expansion in the flow of capital, especially from developed countries, into low- and middle-income national economies (characteristic of most Caribbean nations) is one critically important and often touted feature of this world-wide development and a not-so-subtle underlying "moral" message about how to be a beneficiary among the primary capital-actors in the achievement of human progress.

Accompanying metaphors like "trade flows" are literary elements of the descriptions of "repositioning" accelerated by regional trade agreements such as NAFTA, GATT, and the World Trade Organization. As one delves into the literature of this dimension of professional jargon and symbolism, a new recurring theme is highlighted: developing nations exporting to other developing nations with lower shares of developed-country exports to developing economies than in the past. A positivist spin underlies the conclusion backed up with statistical charts. However, further elaboration of the trade-balance theme reveals that exports estimated to have increased almost 7% annually in low-income economies between 1980 and 1992 likely reflect less real positive development for Caribbean countries and the mass base of their citizens as higher growth in exports occurred in South East Asian countries ("The Asian Tigers" Minidragons: Hong Kong, Taiwan, Singapore, and South Korea among other Asian countries assuming distinction as the world's most dynamic capitalist region). Further interrogation of the theme uncovers that relatively heavy protectionism of primary commodities, particularly agriculture, upon which so much of Caribbean economies is based, has in the past and continues in the present to undermine development and national sovereignty in regions like the Caribbean. The aforementioned statistical characterization of development is indeed a widely propagated and a well-learned form of cultural discourse that expresses values and aspirations through inanimate terms like "gross national product," "second-income level countries," LDC (less-developed countries) and so on. Admittedly, serious examination of the world view and "ways of knowing" and "ways of doing" encapsulated in the jargon of neo-liberal global policies is a sine qua non for deep understanding of the human condition on national, regional, and global scales. So, this distinct "cultural environment" is not to be dismissed, or taken lightly, if the more pervasive and diverse dimensions of human culture are to be fully grasped as an underrecognized and underutilized resource in forging U.S.-Caribbean relations.

Recognition of the importance of geopolitical and economic narratives and imaging should not, however, dissuade, at least, a passing critique of those who dwell solely in that dimension. Socially distant (sometimes alienated) intellectuals and politicians tend to obscure real-life values, aesthetics, and hopes of the mass of their fellow citizens by adopting and often perpetuating macroeconomic worldviews and the accompanying statistically coded social values, leaving out the joyous and sorrowful expressions and creative developmental capacities of common women and men. The daily, year-in and year-out material production and creative expressions of individuals, families, and local communities—born of human yearnings to craft or at least be an active participant in the social, spiritual, and economic development of their nations—are displaced in the minds of the politicians and development community by the sweeping rhetoric of their own trades and imaginations. They frequently drone on in the elaborations of macro and micro indicators, enraptured in the aesthetics of the literature, the flowing metaphors, and crisp logic of the multifaceted global economy.

Who are the main characters of this story? And, what does all of this economic stuff have to do with the generally perceived "soft" topic of culture? Why discuss culture, in the first place, in a setting on geopolitical relations, immigration, and regional and international economics in the Caribbean? The relevance of these new global economic developments to the subject of repositioning of U.S.-Caribbean relations is on the surface rather obvious, even to those whose knowledge of the field of international economics is nominal. Basic terms like "trade balances," "investment capital," "underdevelopment," "industrialization," and "sustainable development" are calmly accepted as common parlance even though the human story lines (social relations) they reflect are problematic. The language of development tends to generalize and make abstract complex social realities and to a certain extent avoid and/or obscure human agency—human spirit!

Nevertheless, the language and narratives of international economics and politics are critically important in vetting the topic of culture. What is usually missing is critical examination of the cultural values inherent in the reigning paradigms. Little or no mention is made of the objective distinctions and to some degree clashes between an elite disciplinary jargon and the intrinsic vibrant expressions of everyday life where the majority of the people of the nation or the region are making micro-decisions about employment, household expenditures, long-term education plans, festivals, and other life issues that are embedded in macro-economic realities. Are the macro-thinkers and planners unaware or simply dismissive of the concomitant cultural dimensions of the new global society? The question is especially pertinent to Caribbean and U.S. politicians, economists, development specialists, and other related professionals, including artists and cultural workers more broadly, whose backgrounds are rooted in the African-Caribbean-American heritages and working class realities of the American hemisphere. Do the "cultural energies" so critical to survival and progress at whatever scale achieved by the vast populations of Caribbean peoples have to be left out of global development paradigms? Where do categorizations of "cultural flows and adaptations," "cultural capital," "cultural imperialism," and "cultural democracy" fit into the topic of repositioning U.S.-Caribbean relations? The questions about cultural terms are not posed to be answered in this paper, but rather they are posed to belie the sterility of neoliberal economic language and to invoke our attention and sensibilities to the massive, complex humanity that professional development culture tends to ignore. Millions of working people underlie the discussions of international economic indicators and policies. They constitute, in all their national, ethnic, racial, gender, and class distinctions, the all-too-often unaddressed/unlistened to humanity ("labor" and "consumer base" in another mode of cultural communication) in which economic models, trade agreements, and theories of growth and development are rooted.

The estimated 200 million combined population of ACS members (the thirteen CARICOM nations, Central American States, the nations of Cuba, Colombia, the Dominican Republic, Haiti, Mexico, Suriname, Venezuela, and the fifteen dependent territories, that comprise ACS Associate membership) represent a sizable mass and diversity of human cultures as well as of human labor and consumers—an estimated $500 billion gross product negotiated in everyday life through several languages and religious, aesthetic, and intellectual traditions.

The new global economic realties are no doubt lowering (some would argue undermining) the vertical importance of the nation-state and transforming it into regional economic and political identities that would in some logical sense further lower the significance of national politics and national values. Caribbean leaders and citizens periodically express concern about the penetration of U.S. culture and the consequent devaluing of indigenous cultural expression. Valid as the concerns are, we are also witnessing in the post-Cold War era a contrary trend characterized by a heightened sense of national, ethnic, religious, and race-based notions of culture that privileges national/cultural origins as the foundation of transnational identities. Samuel P. Huntington's none-too-charitable explanations and rather ominous, if not hyperbolic, warnings about "a clash of civilizations" and "multiculturalism" on a world scale are useful to the extent that they reflect the emergence of culture as a concomitant policy category that must be factored into understanding economic trends of global capitalism.

In the case of the ACS, one need but peruse the list of culturally distinct countries to see that questions of language, literature, religion, style, social values, cultures of work, social cohesion, and social schisms, among other received aesthetic and humanistic traditions and practices, reflect a broad culturally diverse populace rendered abstract in the terminology and discussions of global economics and regional political and trade organizations. In effect, the trumpeting of neoliberal development terminology and indicators drowns out and blocks from view the literal sounds and lived behaviors of the racially and culturally diverse, class differentiated, gendered realities of territorial citizens and a-spatial, transnational cultural communities.

An obvious underestimation, or maybe disdain, for the general populace pervades the economic logic that tacitly or overtly asserts that ascendancy in exports, balance of trade surplus, and similar indicators are tantamount to the well-being of the whole of a nation's people. Cultural workers and development professionals alike should be concerned that the rather fluid, axiomatic articulation of economic and policy analysts renders their concepts, theories, and equations socially unaccountable as they convey false synonymy between elite business and political circles and mass identity.

The need as well as the desire for economic development are so powerful among ACS nations that the ACS faces tremendous risks of not recognizing the integral importance of culture in development and the importance of a conscious and carefully crafted approach to culture as policy category that can stimulate and infuse development activities with the spirit and vast practical energies of everyday citizens.

Historically, progressive Commonwealth Caribbean leaders like former Jamaican Prime Minister Michael Manley have touted the ACS as "a prospect of integrating productive, financing, and marketing capacity."[1] Who, however, has raised the advantages of recognizing and capitalizing on the trans-Caribbean and trans-American exchanges, adoptions, and adaptations of culture that invariably accompany the increasing movement of diverse cultural groups represented in the ACS? What will be the role of CARIFEST (Caribbean Arts Festival) in fostering the goals of ACS and tempering them so as to relate to the economic and spiritual interests and needs of the distinct cultural ACS populations? What advantage is to be taken of the extension of the Afro-English Caribbean into New York City? What cultural guidance with respect to development activities is to be drawn from the example of Miami-based Cuban,' defeat of an "English-Only" bill, or the election to Congress of Nydia Velaquez, former director of the New York-based Office of the Commonwealth of Puerto Rico?

Bill Thornton, Mayor of San Antonio, Texas, commenting on the "English-Plus" resolution passed in 1995 by the City Council stated, "The international business we bring in will be between countries with two languages. Why would we want to lose something helpful to our community, that will bring in jobs?"[2] The point of the U.S.-Mexico example to be emphasized with respect to U.S.-Caribbean relations is that national and regional cultural expressions are closely linked in their spatial movement (for example, immigration and electronic communications) and influence with global economics and politics. The U.S. Supreme Court ruling recognizing Santeria (the Yoruba-based and fastest growing religion in Cuba since 1959) as a legitimate and thus legally protected religion is but one salient reflection of the "social power" of Caribbean culture in the United States and, by implication, the political and economic power of other aspects of culture on an increasingly economically integrated world.

Whether it be the cultural matters described earlier that relate to the Caribbean or more-ominous cases—like Bosnia, where cultural clashes resonate in politics and the economics of military arrangements—it should be clear that arenas of national and international politics and economics should not be left to specialists alone. When international relations are pursued without sufficient regard for cultural and social factors, the souls and spirits of everyday people are too often crushed and reconstituted into mechanical cogs of an ever-expanding economic system that values them only, or mostly, as commodities, then despises their morals and social behaviors. The economic position of many women make this sorry case in the economic growth in Asia, especially in China; and ironically, the tourism-related prostitution of Socialist Cuba is the human downside of an upturn in Cuban economic indicators. The brain drain (nurses and intellectuals) from the English-speaking Caribbean is another example of economic pulls inherent in the history of U.S.-Caribbean relations. Remittances from Caribbean-American citizens and residents in the United States to families "back home in the Caribbean" on the other hand express positive transnational cultural ties and identities that should be factored into regional definitions and international relations as cultural capital to be positively exploited. As would be the case of bauxite, or sugar, or nutmeg, Cuba has above all the Caribbean countries publicized and exploited Afro-Caribbean culture in relation to the United States and Canada.

The emergence of cultural factors on par with politics, economics, military considerations, and international relations in general should command the attention of cultural workers in universities, museums, libraries, community-based programs, and organizations and motivate them to join with policymakers and institutions organized expressly to address regional and hemispheric economic integration and development. We should heed the findings of the UNESCO report "Our Creative Diversity" of the World Commission on Culture and Development, which states, "Development divorced from its human or cultural context is growth without a soul. Economic development in its full flowering is part of a people's culture."

If in relation to development and the economy, as the UNESCO report goes on to state, "culture's role is not exhausted as a servant of ends but is the social basis of the ends themselves," what are the implications for the ACS with respect to arguably the least recognized cultural groups among their nations—African-Caribbean-Americans? The question is posed with acknowledgment of the changing definitions of the Caribbean over time to encompass parts of Central America and South America (consider the aforementioned references to "a-spatial" cultural communities and to the "New York Caribbean"). However, whether it be a traditional view or expanded geographical approach as in the case of ACS membership, African-American cultural realities and needs have been almost studiously avoided and/or obscured in regional and hemispheric policy circles. Indigenous communities have received far more recognition with respect to the implications of their cultural distinctions for political, social, educational, and cultural development than have the millions of African-Caribbean-American inhabitants of Colombia, Cuba, Dominican Republic, Costa Rica, Venezuela, and so on. As the flow of exports and capital increases among the nations of the ACS, no doubt the flow of citizens and diverse cultural values will also. Ideological or cultural identification is more advanced, at least among intellectuals and cultural workers of the various African-Caribbean-American communities, resulting from international literary conferences and journals, comparative studies of African-influenced religions, Creole languages, and the like. Yet, little has been done to focus and activate attention around the inadequate material conditions of life and racism suffered by the vast majority of African-Caribbean-Americans. However, I think we can expect more transnational identification, communication, organization, and cooperation (among cultural communities in different countries and, to a limited but noticeable extent in the near future, more identification and activity among and between national leaders) directed to material and educational development of those communities wherever they exist in the hemisphere. In the past few years, U.S. foundations, media (mainstream and racial/cultural-African diasporic-focused), African-American colleges and universities, and the United States Information Agency/Service have given more attention to and/or sponsored more visits to the United States by Afro-Latin politicians, journalists, women, and community leaders.

How development specialists and cultural workers concerned with U.S.-Caribbean relations will engage this arena is yet to be determined. There should be no question that the time to bridge these two sectors and mold culturally informed development has arrived. The big question is will Caribbean leadership on both sides of the present divide acknowledge and explore the vibrancy and relevant cultural resources for development in African-Caribbean-American cultural life, or will neo-liberal development policies and U.S. grounded cultural values maintain hegemony and be adopted wholesale? A repositioning (and a reformulation) between the cultural values of state leadership in political and economic spheres and the aspirations, values, and needs espoused by the mass social base they claim to represent is a prerequisite, or at least, simultaneous step, to fashion U.S.-Caribbean relations that will reflect and respond to those diverse sensibilities of Caribbean citizens and resist the dangers of cultural imperialism and homogenization that flow with globalization.

NOTES

1. "Regional Integration: Caribbean Hopes," *Cuba Business*. Vol. 8., No. 6, July-August, 1994.

2. *Open Dialogue*, Newsletter of the Association of American Cultures. Vol. 8. No. 6, p. 4.

Selected Bibliography

Baptiste, Fitzroy A. 1988. "The Exploitation of Caribbean Bauxite and Petroleum, 1914–1945." *Social and Economic Studies* 37, nos. 1–2: 107–42.

Baptiste, Fitzroy A. 1988. *War, Cooperation and Conflict: The European Possessions in the Caribbean, 1939–1945.* Westport, CT: Greenwood Press.

Bennett, William J. 1994 "Immigration: Making Americans." *The Washington Post,* December 4.

Bodnar, John. 1985. *The Transplanted: A History of Immigrants in Urban America.* Bloomington: Indiana University Press.

Brian, Elliot, and David MacLennan. 1994. "Education, Modernity and Neo-Conservative School Reform in Canada, Britain and the United States." *British Journal of Sociology of Education* 15, no. 2: 165–85.

Brimelow, Peter. 1995. *Alien Nation.* New York: Random House.

Burn, North. 1964. *United States Base Rights in the British West Indies, 1940–1962.* Ph.D. Thesis. Princeton: Fletcher School of Law and Diplomacy.

Camejo, Acton. 1971. "Racial Discrimination in Employment in the Private Sector in Trinidad and Tobago." *Social and Economic Studies* 20, no. 3: 294–318.

Caribbean Tourism Organization. 1994. *Caribbean Tourism Statistical Report: 1993* Edition. Barbados: Caribbean Tourism Organization.

Chernick, Sidney E. 1978. *The Commonwealth Caribbean: The Integration Experience.* Baltimore: Johns Hopkins University Press.

Chisholm, Shirley. 1973. *The Good Fight.* New York: Harper and Row.

———. 1970. *Unbought and Unbossed.* Boston: Houghton Mifflin Company.

Cudjoe, Selwyn. 1990. *Caribbean Women Writers.* Wellesley, MA: Calaloux Publications.

Dalphinis, Morgan. 1985. *Caribbean and African Languages.* London: Karia Press.

Davis, Kortright. 1990. *Emancipation Still Comin'.* New York: Orbis.

Deere, Carmen D. et al. 1990. *In the Shadows of the Sun: Caribbean Development Alternatives and U.S. Policy.* Boulder, CO: Westview Press.

Devonish, Hubert. 1986. *Language and Liberation.* London: Karia Press.

Dookhan, Issac. 1985. *The United States in the Caribbean.* London: Collins Caribbean.

Fedarko, Kevin. 1996. "The Cold War Is Back." *Time*, March 11.

Gayle, Dennis, and Jonathan Goodrich, eds. 1993. *Tourism Marketing and Management in the Caribbean.* New York: Routledge.

Gibbons, Rawle. 1995. "Pan in Focus." *Trinidad and Tobago Review* 18, nos. 1–3: 1, 25.

Glazer, Nathan, and Daniel P. Moynihan. 1974. *Beyond the Melting Pot: The Negroes, Puerto Ricans, Jews and the Irish of New York City.* 2nd Edition. Cambridge, MA: MIT Press.

Habermas, J. 1985. "Neo-Conservative Culture Criticism in the United States and Germany: An Intellectual Movement in Political Cultures." In *Habermas and Modernity*, edited by R. Berstein. Cambridge, MA: MIT Press.

Holder, Calvin. 1980."The Rise and Fall of West Indian Politicians in New York City, 1900–1987." In *Political Behavior and Social Interaction: Caribbean and African American Residents in New York*, edited by George A. Irish and E. W. Riviere. New York: Caribbean Research Center, Medgar Evers College, CUNY.

Huddle, Donald. 1995. *The Net National Costs of Immigration in 1994.* Washington, DC: Carrying Capacity Network.

Kasinitz, Philip. 1992. *Caribbean New York: Black Immigrants and the Politics of Race.* Ithaca, NY: Cornell University Press.

King, Lloyd. 1994. "Cultural Perceptions in the Relations between the Caribbean and Venezuela." *Caribbean Affairs*, July, 58–73.

Kraly, Ellen P. 1987. "U.S. Immigration Policy and the Immigrant Populations of New York." In *New Immigrants in New York*, edited by Nancy Foner. New York: Columbia University Press.

Lalta, Stanley, and Marie Freckleton. 1993. *Caribbean Economic Development: The First Generation.* Kingston: Ian Randle Publishers.

Le Franc, Elsie, ed. 1994. *Consequences of Structural Adjustment: A Review of the Jamaican Experience.* Barbados: Canoe Press.

Lewis, Gordon K. 1968. *The Growth of the Modern West Indies.* New York: Monthly Review Press.

———. 1987. *Grenada: The Jewel Despoiled.* Baltimore and London: Johns Hopkins University Press.

Mandle, Jay R. 1996. *Persistent Underdevelopment: Change and Economic Modernization in the West Indies.* New York: Gordon and Breach.

Manigat, Leslie. 1976. "The Year in Perspective (From the late 1950's to 1975: The Emergence of the Caribbean on the International Scene)." In *The Caribbean Yearbook of International Relations.* Leyden and Trinidad and Tobago: The Institute of International Relations, University of the West Indies.

Manning, Frank E. 1990. "Overseas Caribbean Carnivals: The Art and Politics of a Transnational Celebration." In *Plantation Society in the Americas,* edited by Thomas M. Fiehrer and Michael W. Loderick. New Orleans: T. Ficher.

McAfee, Kathy. 1991. *Storm Signals: Structural Adjustment and Development Alternatives in the Caribbean.* Boston: South End Press.

Mills, Charles W. 1993. "A Comment on Race, Class and Gender—The Unholy Trinity." In *Race, Class and Gender in the Future of the Caribbean,* edited by J. Edward Greene. Kingston: Institute of Social and Economic Research, University of the West Indies.

Moore, Carlos. 1988. *Castro, the Blacks and Africa.* Los Angeles: Center for Afro-American Studies, University of California.

Nettleford, Rex M. 1978. *Caribbean Cultural Identity: The Case of Jamaica, an Essay in Cultural Dynamics.* Kingston: Institute of Jamaica.

North, David S., and Judy A. Whitehead. 1991. "Policy Recommendations for Improving the Utilization of Emigrant Resources in Eastern Caribbean Nations." *Small Country Development and International Labor Flows,* edited by Anthony P. Maingot. Boulder, CO: Westview Press.

Nossiter, Adam. 1995. "A Jamaican Way Station in the Bronx." *The New York Times,* October 25, Section B.

Palacio, Joseph O. 1990. *Socioeconomic Integration of Central American Immigrants in Belize.* Mexico City: Cubola Productions.

Palmer, Ransford W. 1990. *In Search of a Better Life: Perspectives on Migration from the Caribbean.* New York: Praeger.

———. 1995. *Pilgrims from the Sun: West Indian Migration to America.* New York: Twayne Publishers.

Parris, Carl. 1975. "Chaguaramas Revisited." In *The Caribbean Yearbook of International Relations*. Trinidad: Institute of International Relations, University of the West Indies.

———. 1985. "Power and Privilege in Trinidad & Tobago." *Social and Economic Studies* 34, no. 2: 97–109.

Pérez, Luis A., Jr. 1986. "Politics, Peasants and People of Color: The 1912 'Race War' in Cuba Reconsidered." *Hispanic American Historical Review* 66, no. 3: 509–39.

Primo Braga, Carlos A. 1995. "Trade-Related Intellectual Property Issues: The Uruguay Round Agreement and its Economic Implications." In *The Uruguay Round and the Developing Economies*, edited by Will Martin and L. Alan Winters. World Bank Discussion Papers #307. Washington, DC: The World Bank.

Purdy, Matthew. 1994. "Parade Shows Off West Indian Political Clout." *New York Times*, September 6, B3-1.

Richardson, Bonham C. 1992. *The Caribbean in the Wider World, 1492–1992: A Regional Geography*. New York: Cambridge University Press.

Ryan, Selwyn. 1991. *The Muslimeen Grab for Power: Race, Religion and Revolution in Trinidad and Tobago*. Port of Spain, Trinidad: Imprint Caribbean.

Ryan, Selwyn, and Taimoon Stewart, eds. 1994. *Entrepreneurship in the Caribbean: Culture, Structure, Conjuncture*. St. Augustine, Trinidad: Institute of Social and Economic Research, University of the West Indies.

Said, Edward. 1993. *Culture and Imperialism*. New York: Vintage Books.

Smith, M. G. 1965. *The Plural Society in the West Indies*. Berkeley and Los Angeles: University of California Press.

Smith, Raymond T. 1967. "Social Stratification, Cultural Pluralism and Integration in West Indian Societies." In *Caribbean Integration: Papers on Social, Political and Economic Integration*, edited by Sybil Lewis and Thomas G. Matthews. Rio Piedras, Puerto Rico: Institute of Caribbean Studies.

Sowell, Thomas. 1975. *Race and Economics*. New York: David McKay Co.

———. 1978. *Essays and Data on American Ethnic Groups*. Washington, DC: The Urban Institute.

Taylor, Frank F. 1993. *To Hell with Paradise: A History of the Jamaican Tourist Industry*. Pittsburgh: University of Pittsburgh Press.

Thomas, Clive Y. 1988. *The Poor and the Powerless: Economic Policy and Change in the Caribbean*. New York: Monthly Review Press.

Tomasson, Robert. 1971. "A Festival in Brooklyn Salutes West Indians With Calypso Beat." *New York Times*, September 6, 23.

Ueda, Reeda. "West Indians." 1980. In *Harvard Encyclopedia of American Ethnic Groups*, edited by Stephan Thernstrom et al. Cambridge, MA: Harvard University Press.

United States Bureau of the Census. 1990. *Profiles of Our Ancestry: Selected Characteristics by Ancestry Group*. CPH-L-149, Washington, DC: Government Printing Office.

West Indian Commission. 1992. *Time for Action*. Blackrock, Barbados: The West Indian Commission.

White, Averille. 1988. "Eastern Caribbean Migrants in the USA: A Demographic Profile." *Bulletin of Eastern Caribbean Affairs* 13, no. 4.

The World Bank. 1993. *Caribbean Region: Access, Quality and Efficiency in Education*. Washington, DC: World Bank.

Young, Alma, and Dion E. Phillips, eds. 1986. *Militarization in the Non-Hispanic Caribbean*. Boulder, CO: Lynne Rienne Publishers.

Index

Acker Group BWIA, 27–29, 48n.33
ACS. *See* Association of Caribbean States
Activism, arts and, 120–21
African-American community: interest in Caribbean transformation, 113; as sibling constituency, 126
African-American politicians, and Labor Day Carnival, 92
African-Caribbean Americans: ACS recognition of, 148–49; migration of, 42–43
African-Cubans, US treatment of, 23
African religions, 39, 42, 133–34
Afro-beat, commoditization of, 38–39
Agricultural Utilization Agreements, 24–25
Aircraft: as first ICBMs, 13–16; naval, 13, 15

Air travel, 13, 27–29, 55
Alienation, in Caribbean, 131–32, 138
Alien Registration Act, 77
Aluminum. *See* Bauxite
Aluminum Company of America (ALCOA), 16
Aluminum Company of Canada (ALCAN), 16
"American Lake" strategic triangle, 11–12
Americas, culture of, 102–4, 108–9, 113–14
Anarchist Act, 77
And the Dish Ran Away with the Spoon, 5, 119–20
Antigua: migration from, 56; tourism in, 55; and US, 18, 23, 24, 25
Arts: and activism, 120–21; regional integration of, 107
Aruba, defined as Caribbean, 98

About the Editor and Contributors

FITZROY A. BAPTISTE is Professor of History at the University of the West Indies, Trinidad.

MERLE COLLINS is Professor of English at the University of Maryland at College Park.

KORTRIGHT DAVIS is Professor of Theology in the School of Divinity at Howard University.

JAMES EARLY is Director of Cultural Communications at the Smithsonian Institution's Center for Folklife Program and Cultural Studies.

JAY R. MANDLE is W. Bradford Wiley Professor of Economics at Colgate University.

ERROL MILLER is Professor of Teacher Education at the University of the West Indies, Jamaica.

RANSFORD W. PALMER is Professor of Economics at Howard University.

JOYCE TONEY is Assistant Professor in the Department of Black and Puerto Rican Studies at Hunter College.

CURTIS A. WARD is an attorney with the law firm of Curtis Ward Associates in Silver Spring, Maryland.

ISBN 0-275-95859-0

HARDCOVER BAR CODE